# MAKING THE MASTERS

**Also by David Barrett:**

*Golf Magazine's Golf Rules Explained*

*Golf Courses of the U.S. Open*

*Golfing with Dad*

*Golf's Dream 18s*

*Miracle at Merion*

*The PGA Championship: 1916–1985* (contributor)

*Golf In America: The First 100 Years* (contributor)

*Golf the Greatest Game: The USGA Celebrates Golf in America*
(contributor)

*20th Century Golf Chronicle* (contributor)

*Golf Legends of All Time* (contributor)

*The Wit & Wisdom of Golf* (contributor)

*Best of Golf* (contributor)

*These Guys Are Good* (contributor)

*The Love of Golf* (contributor)

# MAKING THE MASTERS

BOBBY JONES AND THE BIRTH OF
AMERICA'S GREATEST GOLF TOURNAMENT

## DAVID BARRETT

SKYHORSE PUBLISHING

Skyhorse Publishing books may be purchased in bulk at special discounts for sales promotion, corporate gifts, fund-raising, or educational purposes. Special editions can also be created to specifications. For details, contact the Special Sales Department, Skyhorse Publishing, 307 West 36th Street, 11th Floor, New York, NY 10018 or info@skyhorsepublishing.com.

Skyhorse® and Skyhorse Publishing® are registered trademarks of Skyhorse Publishing, Inc.®, a Delaware corporation.

Visit our website at www.skyhorsepublishing.com.

10 9 8 7 6 5 4 3 2 1

Library of Congress Cataloging-in-Publication Data is available on file.

ISBN: 978-1-61608-609-1

Printed in the United States

For Luda, Michael, and Sophia, and for my mom, Virginia

# CONTENTS

The first Masters was won by Horton Smith, a top-notch player once hailed as the next Bobby Jones. The second was won by Sarazen, probably the best player, and certainly the biggest star, of the day.

Sarazen won that 1935 tournament thanks largely to holing a shot from 230 yards for a double eagle, a feat so spectacular it was called the "Shot Heard Round the World." This served to spread Masters fame far and wide and helped to sustain the standing of the tournament even as it was clear that Jones would not be a competitive threat.

The tournament was held on a course co-designed by Jones and Alister MacKenzie, one which rapidly earned a reputation as one of the best in the country. Its design, which challenged the best players in the world while also allowing for heroics like Sarazen's, proved perfect for producing the kind of excitement that would help the tournament become the most-watched golf event in the world once the television era came along.

The humble aspects mostly stemmed from the fact that Augusta National and the Masters were launched during the Depression, hardly the best time to start such ventures. And besides, golf wasn't then the big deal it later became. Tournaments didn't draw anything near the galleries they do today—a thousand was a good crowd—and $5,000 purses were the norm.

It's fascinating to look back on those origins from today's perspective when Masters tickets are the hardest to obtain in sports and people all over the globe gather in front of television sets to watch the pictures beamed from Augusta each spring. But it's important to remember that its early difficulties were more than offset by factors that made the Masters an immediate success and ultimately into the spectacle that it is today.

Even when the Masters was little, it was big.

# MAKING THE MASTERS

# 1

# THE FOUNDERS/BOBBY AND CLIFF

**B**OBBY JONES AND CLIFFORD Roberts were a study in contrasts.

Jones grew up in a stable environment, a son of Atlanta whose family rented a summer house outside the city at East Lake, where Bobby learned to play golf.

Roberts's family moved more times than anyone could count when he was growing up, living in various towns in Iowa, Kansas, California, Oklahoma, and Texas; his father was "always interested in what was on the other side of the next hill," as Roberts recalled.

Jones was from an upper middle class background; his father was a lawyer.

Roberts wasn't poor growing up, but his family's fortunes ebbed and flowed.

Jones was an only child whose parents gave him all of the attention and encouragement he needed without spoiling or smothering him. His father ended up being his best friend for life.

Roberts was one of five children. His father was often away from home; his mother had many health problems and committed suicide when Cliff was nineteen.

Jones had bachelor's degrees from Georgia Tech and Harvard and passed the Georgia bar exam after attending Emory University law school. He was smart in a way that allowed him to shine academically, whether studying engineering, literature, or law.

Roberts quit school at the age of fifteen and in the ensuing years scratched out an existence as a traveling clothing salesman. He was smart, but in a savvy, street-smart kind of way.

Jones was known for his modesty and had a polite, gentlemanly quality about him. He spent a couple of years in the real estate business, but didn't enjoy selling. He became a lawyer, but stayed away from the courtroom, instead concentrating on providing legal advice and working with contracts.

Roberts could be blunt; he knew exactly what he wanted and let nothing or no one stand in his way. He could be very persuasive, and was a very successful salesman.

Jones's golfing accomplishments made him one of the most famous athletes of the 1920s, a decade of athletic heroes. In fact, he was one of the most famous *people* in America.

Roberts wasn't famous himself, but he was fascinated with famous people and an avid reader of biographies. After arriving in New York and getting involved in the investment business, he moved comfortably in a world of highly successful businessmen.

The two weren't anything alike. But together they created one of the nation's elite golf clubs—Augusta National—and a golf tournament that leads the world in prestige—the Masters. Neither Bobby nor Cliff would have had a chance of accomplishing either feat by himself.

Augusta National was all about Bobby Jones. It was his idea, his dream. But he needed someone with Roberts's iron will and business acumen to turn it into reality. The Masters was Roberts's idea. But without the involvement and name of Jones, it would have been just another tournament instead of one that almost instantaneously achieved major status.

Jones was an exalted figure when he retired from competitive golf at the age of twenty-eight. While he is still considered one of the greatest to ever play the game, his accomplishments may be underappreciated today when you consider the following astonishing statistics.

During his short career, Jones entered thirty-one national championships (U.S. Open, British Open, U.S. Amateur, British Amateur) and won thirteen. All of those thirteen victories came after he turned twenty-one in 1923—and they came in only twenty-one tries.

That's a winning percentage of almost 62 percent from 1923 on. With four runner-up finishes, that means he finished either first or second nearly 81 percent of the time in national championships.

His record in open championships (seven wins in eleven tries after 1923) was even a little better than in amateur championships (six wins in ten tries in that span). The competition wasn't as strong in the amateur events, but the match-play format used in those tournaments is always a bit of a crapshoot.

Stretching it back to 1922, in his last nine U.S. Opens he finished first four times, second four times, and eleventh once. He entered three British Opens and won every one. That's eleven top-two finishes in his last twelve national open appearances, with seven wins. Extraordinary.

He did all this while competing essentially in his spare time. He never entered more than a couple other competitions a year other than the national championships—sometimes none at all. There were only three years when he played in all four championships—1921, 1926, and 1930. Those were the years he made the overseas trip for the British Amateur and British Open; he made a special trip for just

Chattanooga, Tennessee, and Hendersonville, North Carolina, at the same time, but showed his special affinity for Augusta by enrolling his son, Fleetwood (for whom his hotels were named) at Richmond Academy there. The Commodore, as he liked to be called, was so enamored with the potential of Augusta that he predicted its population would grow from 60,000 to 250,000 in the next twenty-five years.

The announcement led to a land boom along the soon-to-be-paved Washington Road. Various parcels in the vicinity of the proposed hotel, sited four miles from downtown in a sparsely populated area, were snatched up by both local and out-out-town speculators in a frenzied three-week period. Real estate companies ran large ads in the *Augusta Chronicle*. One advertised 9.9 acres about a quarter mile from the Fleetwood for $1,550 an acre, saying "We Have Option Until Noon Today." Another advertised 200 acres four miles away for $70 an acre. "Within less than one year when this tract is sold for from $500 to $1,000 per acre do not say 'I could have bought it for $70.' This is for Only One Week and May be Sold Today to SOMEBODY ELSE if YOU WAIT."

Ground was broken in February 1926, with the hotel expected to be ready by the following January. It would be a year-round hotel, not just a winter resort, and would feature entertainment designed to draw local young people and make it a hot spot.

The golf component was not nearly as important to Stoltz as it would later be to Jones. The Commodore announced that the engineer for the construction of the hotel would also lay out the golf course—an indication that a masterpiece along the lines of what Alister MacKenzie later created was probably not in the offing.

The hotel foundation was laid, but work halted while a mile-long spur was built from the main railroad line to bring materials directly to the site. Work never resumed.

It has often been written that the Commodore's Augusta plans were ruined when a severe hurricane hit Miami in September 1926, severely damaging the Fleetwood Hotel and ultimately sending Stoltz into bankruptcy. A good story, but it's not true. Actually, he backed out of building the hotel months earlier.

A legal notice dated May 13 that ran in June in the *Chronicle* stated that Stoltz was required to appear in Richmond County Superior Court "to make answer to the equitable petition of Washington Heights Development Company against you for the cancellation of the contract entered into by said company and yourself on January 23, 1926, whereby you agreed to construct a hotel on said property near Augusta, Georgia."

The story was not pursued by the newspaper, but it's a good assumption that Stoltz's reason for abandoning the project was that he was overextended in trying to build three expensive hotels at the same time. So, it was hubris, not a hurricane, that brought the project down. (Stoltz's company did indeed ultimately go bankrupt.)

If the Fleetwood had been built, Jones would have had to find a site for his course elsewhere, maybe in Augusta or maybe somewhere else. And even with the minds of Jones and MacKenzie on the case, it's unlikely the result would have been quite as good as the Augusta National we know today—for the magnificent site gives the place a large part of its charm and the course a large part of its interest.

That site has a long history, stretching back to Indian days. What would become Washington Road leading past the course started out as an Indian trail, and at some point there was an Indian settlement on the property—a burial mound was found during construction of the 12th green. However, it turns out there's probably no truth to the long-told story about Spanish explorer Hernando de Soto meeting Indians there, as recent scholarship no longer has de Soto's route going through what is now Augusta.

15

and stock to cover construction on the Washington Heights Development-owned property. The *Chronicle* pointed out that in addition to the benefits of another resort hotel, it would help real estate prices in the area. An approximate total of $1,250,000 had been invested in the vicinity of the proposed Fleetwood in 1925, and the value of that property had plunged to about 25 percent of that amount.

(The investors came out all right only if they were able to hold on long enough. Over the course of the next thirty years, the area became heavily developed as Augusta grew westward and Washington Road was the main way out of town in that direction.)

Nothing ever came of the hotel idea, presumably because it became clear the money could not be raised. Then in the fall of 1929 the stock market crashed, signaling the start of the Great Depression.

Now Washington Heights Development was stuck with the Berckmans site and another piece of property across Washington Road, with little hope of selling or developing either one as the national and local economy soured. It refurbished part of the manor house and opened it as the Fruitland Manor Tea Room in 1930 and 1931, but that was a small-scale project compared to what was needed for Washington Heights to recoup its investment.

Enter Bobby Jones and Clifford Roberts. Depression or not, Jones was determined to build his dream club and Roberts was determined to help him. The Bon Air-Vanderbilt Company put down $5,000 for a six-month option to buy the property, a decision probably made by vice president Thomas Barrett, giving Roberts time to get everything together.

Roberts formed a group consisting of himself, Barrett, their friend Walton H. Marshall, Fielding Wallace (one of Augusta's most prominent businessmen and president of Augusta Country Club), and Bobby Jones's father, Robert P. Jones, creating a real estate company named the Fruitland Manor Corporation. Fruitland Manor bought the land in late June for $15,000 in cash and assumption of about $60,000 in debt, mostly a first mortgage, according to David Owen's *The Making of the Masters*, the authorized history of Augusta National. (The price reported in the newspaper was $70,000.)

It was a good price. Washington Heights Development had purchased the land across the road for about $500 an acre in 1925, and the Berckmans property probably cost them more than that. Now Fruitland Manor was getting the old Berckmans land for around $200 an acre. However, that benefit, as Jones and Roberts would discover, was offset by the difficulty of trying to build a course and start a golf club during the Depression.

Meanwhile, Jones had to choose an architect for his course. He knew just who he wanted—and it wasn't Donald Ross, the Southeast's most prominent golf architect. Ross had redesigned Augusta Country Club and designed the course of the Forrest-Ricker Hotel that opened in Augusta in 1927. Rumors have reverberated through the decades that Ross was deeply disappointed not to get the Augusta National job. Instead he threw himself into a redesign of his North Carolina masterpiece, Pinehurst's No. 2 Course.

Jones's choice was Dr. Alister MacKenzie, a globe-trotting Scottish architect who had recently settled in the United States, albeit a long way from Augusta in California. The two had met in Scotland at St. Andrews, either during the 1926 Walker Cup or 1927 British Open, an acquaintance they renewed when Jones played in the 1929 U.S. Amateur at Pebble Beach.

On that trip to California, Jones played MacKenzie's new Cypress Point, a Monterey Peninsula masterpiece still ranked among the very best courses in America, and another MacKenzie course up the coast, Pasatiempo. By that time, Jones had in mind that he would someday build his own course, and he decided that MacKenzie was the man to design it.

It wasn't just that Jones was impressed with Cypress Point. He also realized from discussions with MacKenzie and from reading his 1920 book *Golf Architecture* (MacKenzie signed a copy for him) that they shared many ideas about golf design. Primary among them were the beliefs that courses should be designed with the average player in mind and should require a lot of strategy; Jones also liked the way MacKenzie utilized natural features in his designs. And perhaps the most important point of all was that both were inspired by the Old Course at St. Andrews.

MacKenzie, for his part, was a great admirer of Jones. He followed him during the 1927 British Open and later declared that he and his fellow Scotsmen were happier that Jones won than they would have been if a Scot had taken the title. (MacKenzie was born and raised in England, but his parents were Scottish and he considered himself a Scotsman.)

Jones and MacKenzie were both well educated and well rounded, with interests beyond golf. Jones was a licensed lawyer with degrees in engineering and literature, while MacKenzie had been educated as a doctor, though he seemed more interested in acquiring degrees than practicing, and served Great Britain during World War I as an expert in camouflage. Jones must have sensed that because of their rapport and their similar views, MacKenzie would be receptive to his ideas—and enjoyable company, too.

# 3

# THE COURSE/
# DOCTOR'S PRESCRIPTION

---

**A**N ARTICLE IN THE *Augusta Chronicle* of June 30, 1931, reported that Fruitland Manor Corporation had purchased the old Berckmans place, but the paper couldn't secure a statement as to the "aims and purposes" of the corporation. It was only on July 15 that most of Augusta learned that Bobby Jones was behind Fruitland Manor when they read about the announcement that the greatest golfer in the game would be building his dream course in their city.

Again there was a two-line banner headline across the width of the front page of the *Chronicle*, this time in type not quite as large and not in all caps: "Bobby Jones to Build His Ideal Golf Course on Berckmans' Place." If the headline fell slightly short of the Fleetwood Hotel announcement six years earlier, the overall coverage was more intense. There were six lengthy stories and an editorial about the Jones course and club in that day's *Chronicle*.

O. B. Keeler, the Atlanta writer and Jones confidant, predicted that the course "in all probability is to be the most famous layout in

North America, if not in all the world." Keeler was speaking truth, not hype.

Alister MacKenzie was on hand for a three-day visit to walk the property with Jones and refine a routing plan—MacKenzie had made a tentative one based on study of a map and aerial photos during the train trip from New York to Augusta. Also present was a representative of the Olmsted Brothers landscape design firm, which was handling the remainder of the property.

*Chronicle* sports editor Harold Stephens tagged along as Jones and MacKenzie toured the property. Jones's enthusiasm was palpable as he looked down over the site from the hill behind the manor house. "When I come here, I'm going to play some golf!" he said.

The design team walked the mostly open property armed with their maps, photos, and MacKenzie's tentative plan. "Here's a peach of a hole, doctor," Jones was heard to exclaim on one occasion as he envisioned a hole (probably what would become the 13th) proceeding along the edge of the woods to a green next to a creek.

The group set a swift pace under the blazing sun in 93-degree heat. An Augustan accompanying the party had to stretch out in the shade and wait for a car to come take him back to the house, but Jones and the sixty-year-old MacKenzie were unaffected. "I don't see how you stand it bare-headed," someone said to Jones. "My skull's thick," he responded.

Jones released an official announcement that read: "I am joining with a group of friends as one of the organizers of a new club to be known as the Augusta National Golf Club. It is a private undertaking and in no sense a commercial project. Although my time is now largely devoted to the practice of law, golf will always be my hobby, and having retired from active competition, my ambition is to help build something that may be recognized as one of the great courses of the world.

"Augusta, which is in my home state, has been selected for the location because it offers such a splendid winter climate and a golf setting that I consider unsurpassed for the idea we have in mind."

That selection sent Augusta into a frenzy. The *Chronicle* ran a story stringing together quotes from sixteen prominent citizens, all of them extolling Bobby Jones in florid language and saying essentially that this was the greatest news to hit Augusta in years—maybe ever. The primary significance to the city was the boost provided to its standing as a winter golf resort.

Augusta National would draw members from all of the country, many from colder climates who would need a place to stay when they visited in the winter (the club planned to operate only from late fall to early spring). Or they might build a home near the club—real estate values in the vicinity were expected to rise substantially as a winter colony developed. There was also the prestige factor. The publicity generated by Jones's new club was expected to draw people to the city whether they were Augusta National members or not.

"I regard it as the biggest single achievement in the annals of Augusta as a winter resort," said Thomas Barrett. "There is no way to estimate the far reaching effects of the coming hero of Bobby Jones for he numbers his friends and admirers among the men of prominence throughout the nation."

Barrett was an interested observer, as his Bon Air-Vanderbilt was the largest of Augusta's three resort hotels, which stayed open only for the winter season. The Bon Air kicked off Augusta's winter resort ambitions when it opened in 1888, and also introduced a golf component when it rented some land and constructed a nine-hole course for its guests in 1897. Those holes were later incorporated into Augusta Country Club, whose Lake and Hill courses were open to Bon Air guests.

Across the Savannah River in South Carolina, the town of North Augusta had boasted the Hampton Terrace Hotel, which was the largest wooden structure in the world when it opened in 1903 and featured a golf course. President William Howard Taft and many other prominent Americans visited Augusta early in the century, but the glory days were interrupted when the Hampton Terrace burned to the ground in 1916 and the Bon Air did the same in 1921. The Bon Air was reborn in a concrete structure in 1923 as part of the Vanderbilt chain. The Hampton Terrace was never rebuilt, leaving a void that was filled by the opening of the Forrest Hills-Ricker Hotel, a project simultaneous to the aborted Fleetwood. (The two "r's" in Forrest came from the first name of one of the developers of that section of town.)

With a portfolio that also included a smaller resort hotel, the Partridge Inn, and a municipal golf course opened in 1928, the addition of Augusta National left the locals proclaiming, in no uncertain terms, that Augusta was now "the winter golf capital of the nation."

Amid such an enthusiastic reception there was no one voicing any doubts, yet Jones felt compelled to point out in his spoken remarks to reporters that "the project, by the way, has been underwritten in its entirety, and full financial arrangements have been made for carrying out all of our plans. There will be no hitch in the plans, whatever. . . . The links will be ready, I am confident, for play by December 1932, and therefore for the golf season of 1933."

The course did indeed come in on schedule—even ahead of it. But the first part of Jones's statement wasn't correct. According to David Owen's history of Augusta National, it took two years to raise the total of $120,000 in underwriting funds. And in December 1931, with clearing of the course already underway, Clifford Roberts informed MacKenzie that it was uncertain if further construction would ensue immediately. A meeting was scheduled for early January when a decision would be made whether "business conditions" would allow the club to proceed with construction.

Initial efforts at securing underwriting had been reasonably successful. They would have been wildly successful if founding member Alfred S. Bourne, heir of the Singer Sewing Machine Company, hadn't been nearly wiped out by the stock market crash. He told Roberts that he would have been happy to underwrite the whole thing if he still had the resources, but now that he was dependent only on income instead of assets he could afford just $25,000, and he would need a year to come up with that sum. Walton H. Marshall matched that $25,000 and Wallace and Boston businessman William C. Watt each contributed $5,000. Then the fundraising slowed down considerably.

"Neither [Jones] nor I had any idea we would have any difficulty getting a number of people to commit to $5,000, thus to get together the total amount of money needed to build a golf course," Roberts said late in life. "But, as the Depression got worse, a lot of our friends we thought were comfortably fixed began to shrink in number . . . We had a most difficult time."

Enough money came in for construction to get the go-ahead in January. It was reported in the *Chronicle*, without any mention of financial difficulties, that on January 13, Jones authorized contractors to begin grading greens and fairways and installing an irrigation system.

With fundraising efforts realizing diminishing returns, Jones contributed $5,000 in 1932. Roberts was reluctant to ask Jones for money, considering Bobby's name to be his most valuable contribution, but Jones was in a good financial position after his Warner Brothers deal. Roberts didn't contribute, according to Owen. That's probably because Cliff was spending so much time in Augusta that he wasn't generating income at his New York business. He stayed in Augusta from September 1931 all the way through May 1932 to supervise course construction and organization of the club.

MacKenzie came to Augusta in October to refine the plan. We know from articles in the *Chronicle* that at this point the holes were numbered in the same order as they are today. However, a MacKenzie diagram dated November 1931 has the nines reversed, meaning that the course finished on what is now the ninth hole. This configuration was played when the course opened and in 1934 for the first Masters. According to Owen's book, there is documentation that the switch was MacKenzie's idea, the reason perhaps being that the original and current ninth green offers a better view from the clubhouse than the 18th.

Some of the holes changed as the plans developed. On MacKenzie's original sketch, the fifth and 17th holes were long enough to be par fives instead of par fours and the 15th short enough to be a par four instead of a par five. That was probably ripe for adjustment: MacKenzie didn't necessarily like assigning par to holes but he did tend to think of a course as playing to "even fours," which adds up to a par 72, whereas the course as sketched would have been a par 73.

The plan developed during MacKenzie's October visit, as reported by Keeler in an article in the December issue of the *American Golfer*, had the 17th cut down to par four size and the 15th lengthened to a par five. But the fifth was still a par five at 470 yards, while the 13th was listed as a very difficult par four of 440 yards, making the course a par 72 but an unbalanced one with nines of 37 and 35. (The holes are referred to by their present numbers here.) It was probably during MacKenzie's last visit in March that the 13th was turned into a great risk/reward par five at 480 yards instead of a par four and the fifth shortened to a 440-yard par four.

Roberts was pleased with MacKenzie's selection as architect because the doctor believed in building courses economically. In fact, MacKenzie wouldn't accept an assignment for a course with a budget of more than $100,000, which is what Augusta's happened to be.

Roberts recalled taking MacKenzie to Whippoorwill, a club in Westchester County north of New York City built on rugged terrain that Cliff had joined because a friend owned the place. Roberts had been impressed with a hole that cost $100,000 to build because it required blasting a lot of solid granite. MacKenzie wasn't so impressed.

When the members pressed MacKenzie for an opinion of their course, he responded, "It's quite remarkable," and left it at that. On the drive back to the city, Roberts asked MacKenzie to elaborate. "I meant," the doctor responded, "that it's quite remarkable that anyone could be damn fool enough to build a course on ground that is so obviously unsuitable for golf."

The Augusta National site was very suitable for golf. There was a significant hill leading down from the high point where the clubhouse would be, but not too steep to build golf holes on. Four creeks running through the property could be utilized in the design, though parts of these were piped underground before the course opened. There were some attractive stands of tall pine trees, but since the land had been used as a nursery much of the property had been cleared to grow smaller plants and shrubs.

In fact, it could be said that the Berckmans contributed to the design—existing corridors between stands of tall pines were used for the second, eighth, 10th, 11th, and 18th fairways. These areas had been cleared, as had a large open area eventually occupied by (north to south) the first part of the eighth fairway, the entire seventh, 17th, 15th, and 14th fairways, and last part of the 13th fairway. When the course opened, you could stand behind the manor house and look down that area all the way to the border of the course at the 13th hole. To the west of that, behind a stand of trees, the land that would become the fifth fairway was also devoid of timber, though that area was covered by thicker brush.

"Whoever cleared this land must have had the idea of golf in mind," Jones said on the day he walked the site with MacKenzie.

Clearing out the nursery plantings and the overgrowth that had sprung up in the six years since the nursery closed was the first step in the course-building process. This occurred in November, followed by tree removal in December. Fortunately, only scattered large trees here and there had to be removed; cutting through any significant forest would have taken a lot longer and blown the construction budget.

The clearing was hard work, as was the construction to follow, but with the Depression in full swing it wasn't difficult to find men to do it. Laborers could have been hired for as low as 50 cents a day—sunup to sunset—but Roberts decided to pay a dollar. This thinking went along with what MacKenzie wrote in his book: "Experience has taught us that a few extra cents paid in men's wages is worth many dollars in actual production."

Once construction started, they didn't mess around. A story in the trade journal *Contractors and Engineers Monthly* noted that it was just 124 calendar days from the start of surface construction to the completion of seeding in late May—really, it took just seventy-six working days, since eighteen Sundays and thirty days lost because of wet ground were included in the total. "It is believed that, considering the volume of dirt moved, the foregoing 124 days constitutes an all-time record in golf course construction."

The word "record" is a bit misleading—there's no official ratio for dirt moved versus number of construction days—but no doubt the pace was quick.

A total of 120,000 cubic yards of dirt was moved, a large amount for a course of its time. Why so much? The 12th green, across Rae's Creek, was in a swampy area that needed a lot of dirt to be made into solid ground. The putting surfaces were undulating, often surrounded by mounds, with dips in front of some greens, all of which required earth to be pushed around. The task was made easier by the use of tractors and bulldozers, though the old mule-and-pan method was used, too.

The short construction time served to keep costs down. So did the fact that MacKenzie's design called for only twenty-two bunkers when most courses featured more than a hundred. The name "Bobby Jones" also helped. So eager were people to be involved with Jones's course that Augusta National was able to obtain some materials at or below cost.

On the other hand, other factors worked to push the costs back upward. The fairways were wider than most courses and the greens larger. And Jones insisted on an irrigation system at a time when few courses had them. (Augusta National was fortunate that it was able to tap into a water line running from the Savannah River to the Augusta reservoir that went under the fifth hole.)

In the end, MacKenzie and construction engineer Wendell P. Miller spent just over the originally planned $100,000—but that represented beating the budget since $15,000 in extras and upgrades had been added.

A key moment in the construction came when MacKenzie made his final visit in March. With the land cleared and the course taking shape, Jones was able to hit shots from various spots to help determine the placement of bunkers, turns of doglegs, and so in. Also, MacKenzie was there for the final shaping of the greens, a vital aspect of any course but especially Augusta National.

While Jones was able to test how the layout would play for a top-flight player, that wasn't the sole focus of the design. Augusta National would go on to become America's most famous tournament course, but it wasn't designed to host the Masters—neither Jones nor Mac-Kenzie knew the tournament would exist when they conceived the course. Jones might have had thoughts about potentially hosting a

U.S. Open, which Augusta National inquired about after it opened, but foremost in his mind were the average players who would make up the membership of his club. What's striking about Augusta National is how much consideration the average golfer was given.

"Dr. MacKenzie and I believe that no good golf hole exists that does not afford a proper and convenient solution to the average golfer and the short player, as well as to the most powerful and accurate expert. We are doing our best to combine these factors in our course," Jones told Keeler.

In *Golf Is My Game*, Jones put it this way: "The first purpose of any golf course is to give pleasure, and that to the greatest possible number of players, without respect to their capabilities."

Based on the reaction to the course, they succeeded.

William D. Richardson in the *New York Times* called it "'a golf course for the forgotten man' for the simple reason that in its conception Bobby has gone out of the way to espouse the cause of the golfer whose scores range between 95 and 130!" Richardson was particularly impressed by the low number of bunkers.

"For the ninety man the course really is easy," wrote H. J. Whigham, a former U.S. Amateur champion turned golf architect. "But for the man who thinks he is a champion it suddenly becomes difficult."

As an example, Whigham pointed to the par fives on the back nine, where the elite player could shoot for the green in two but had to execute a difficult long shot over water, while the average player could do fine just by hitting two normal shots and having a relatively easy short third shot over the hazard. (Like many good players, Whigham underestimates the average golfer's propensity for hitting a poor first or second shot and leaving a fairly long third, and also his capacity to dump an "easy" short shot into the hazard, but the point is still well taken.)

Other parts of the plan included giving alternate routes on wide fairways for the mid- and high-handicappers, and placing the hazards in such a way that the expert can gain an advantage by challenging them.

"In designing courses, I give the player all the room in the world in the direction it will do him the least good, and place the bunkers in such position that the player will be rewarded for accuracy and punished for inaccuracy," MacKenzie told the *Chronicle's* Earl T. DeLoach, explaining that the first route was for the "dub" willing to give up a stroke and the latter route for the expert calling for accuracy and sometimes distance, with usually an intermediate route for the average player or the expert electing to play more safely.

Strategy was the key, MacKenzie and Jones agreed, to making the course playable for all levels and also for creating an interesting test that made the player think.

"A course which is constructed with these principles in view must be interesting because it will offer golfers problems which a man may attempt according to his ability," wrote Jones. "It will never become hopeless for the duffer, nor fail to concern and interest the expert. And it will be found, like old St. Andrews, to become more delightful the more it is studied and played."

The designers pointed to specific holes at St. Andrews as their inspiration for several holes at Augusta National, and cited other courses, too. This, unfortunately, led to the mistaken notion that Augusta *replicated* holes from the British Isles, an assertion that often made its way into articles about the course in the very early days.

While Augusta National didn't have any holes that were exact replicas of holes in Scotland, it did have Scottish characteristics, most notably that many holes were designed for run-up shots. Bouncing the ball onto greens is not a part of the pro game today (and was not even all that much a part of the pro game in 1934), but that run-up possibility still exists on several holes to be taken advantage of by the average player while having been eliminated on several others.

At 6,700 yards, Augusta was a fairly long course for its time. The length was built mostly into the par fours. Neither Jones nor Mac-Kenzie favored more than a couple of "drive-and-a-pitch" holes on a given course, and there were only two at Augusta National, the third and seventh as the holes are numbered today. The other eight par fours ranged from 400 to 440 yards, pretty robust for 1934.

The par fives, on the other hand, were relatively short at 480, 485, 500, and 525 yards. Since the longest was downhill, all were reachable by two strong shots. This was very much a Jones philosophy.

"I am not among those who believe that a par-five hole, so called, must be so extremely long, or must have some peculiarity of design or construction, that it can not be reached in two shots," Jones said. "There are a good many of these holes in our championship courses nowadays, and some people appear quite proud of them. But in competition, it means simply that the man who can hit two really great shots is no better off than the man who can hit two good shots; his third is a bit shorter; that is all. Not by any means a fair chance for the expert to invest his superior skill and range in the picking up of a stroke."

Some architects felt differently. A. W. Tillinghast, for example, believed that par fives were supposed to be three-shot holes. Jones's conception has provided more excitement for tournament play over the years.

The combination of reachable par fives and long par fours gave an advantage to long hitters. So did the implementation of one of Mac-Kenzie's fourteen principles, expressed in *Golf Architecture*: "There should be complete absence of the annoyance and irritation caused by the necessity of searching for lost balls."

The fairways were wide, the rough not deep, and the tree areas clear of underbrush. This was done mainly to increase the enjoyment for the average player, but it also served to help the long-but-wild driver. It should be pointed out, however, that there *was* some rough in the early days, just not the kind in which you could lose your ball. From the 1950s through 1999 the area outside the fairways was trimmed to barely above fairway height, but discernible rough existed at the beginning and does so today. A tournament account from 1934 even describes a player as hitting from knee-deep rough—and such rough can be seen in some photographs—but this would have been pretty far from the fairway and the grass wispy enough that finding the ball wouldn't be a problem.

The final part of the formula was to make the greens challenging for the better player.

"With a course as wide-open as needed to accommodate the average golfer, we can only tighten it up by increasing the difficulty around the hole," Jones wrote in 1959. "This we attempt to do during the tournament by placing the flags in more difficult and exacting positions and by increasing the speed of the greens. Additionally, we try to maintain our greens with such a firmness that they will only hold a well-played shot, and not a ball that has been hit without the backspin reasonably to be expected, considering the length of the shot."

This philosophy held from the very beginning. Jones told Keeler back in 1931 that the greens were not to be "kept soaked" as they were at so many American courses and hole locations at the first Masters were so difficult that they elicited howls of complaint,

MacKenzie told Keeler that the expert golfer "will find a greater variety of shots to play than on the usual course designed for championship competition, so-called. He will be required to plan and think—he will have to use his brain, if he has one."

How much of the course can be attributed to Jones and how much to MacKenzie? Each was polite enough to give the other plenty of credit.

"Bob is not only a student of golf, but of golf courses as well, and, while I had known him for years, I was amazed at his knowledge and clear recollection of almost all the famous holes in England and Scotland as well as here in America," MacKenzie wrote in the *American Golfer*. "He has the faculty of retaining a full conception of any golf hole of special interest that has come under his observation, and I was a bit surprised at the keenness with which he is able to analyze and point out both the strength and the weakness of many, many holes which have impressed him. I am convinced that from no one else could I have obtained such help as he has given me in this undertaking."

Jones, for his part, wrote of MacKenzie, "Of course, there was never any question that he was the architect and I was his advisor and consultant. No man learns how to design a golf course simply by playing golf, no matter how well."

Clearly, MacKenzie did the routing plan and was mostly responsible for the conception of the holes. The two basically agreed on the overall vision of the course, so it can't quite be said that MacKenzie was charged with carrying out Jones's vision. In the "vision thing," they were collaborators.

There are a few areas where one can speculate that Jones had an influence. He felt so strongly that par fives should be reachable in two that one can easily see him making this a requirement for his dream course.

Tom Doak, an acclaimed twenty-first-century golf architect who collaborated on a biography of MacKenzie, points to three other aspects of the course that might be attributed more to Jones than the doctor.

- The exceptionally low number of bunkers: MacKenzie's other courses had considerably more sand.
- The overall length of the course: It was the longest that MacKenzie ever designed.

- Downslopes in the drive zone that could be used to gain added distance on a drive hit to the proper side of the fairway: This fit with Jones's philosophy of giving a reward for a properly placed shot rather than a penalty for a poorly placed one.

There's also the matter of the many changes made to Augusta National in the eight decades since its creation. MacKenzie didn't have a say in the alterations, even those made in the early years: He died of a heart attack in January 1934 at the age of sixty-three, never having seen the finished course (he had planned to attend the 1934 Masters).

Nonetheless, MacKenzie was, and still is, the primary man behind the design of Augusta National, whatever influence Jones had at the outset and whatever changes have been made. It's a worthy monument.

As MacKenzie himself said, Augusta National was "my best opportunity, and I believe, my finest achievement."

# 4

# THE CLUB/BORN IN HARD TIMES

**M**EMBERSHIP IN AUGUSTA NATIONAL Golf Club when it was formed late in 1931 was by invitation only. The difference between then and now is that the club was frantically inviting as many people as it could, and getting very few of them to say yes. That might seem hard to believe today, and even harder to believe when you consider that it cost only $350 to join (adjusted for inflation, that's roughly $5,200 in 2012 dollars) and that annual the dues were only $60 (about $900 in 2012 dollars), lower than most other prestigious clubs of the time.

Still, this was the Depression, so money was tight. Many once-wealthy people had suffered enormous losses in the stock market crash and no longer had extra money for joining golf clubs. People were afraid that they might lose their jobs.

Augustans had the option of joining Augusta Country Club, which was open all year while Augusta National was open for less than five months. Atlantans might have felt betrayed by Jones; in any case, they saw no reason to make the 150-mile trip just to play in weather that might be a few degrees warmer in the winter. Northerners who enjoyed winter golf in the South were supposed to form the core of the club. But how many avid golfers in the early 1930s could afford to spend a considerable part of their winter on vacation? Was it worth it if you could only make it south for a couple of shorter trips? You also had to factor in the cost of traveling to and staying in Augusta, making membership not such a bargain.

Even considering all the potential drawbacks, the level of the club's futility in attracting members, as related by David Owen in *The Making of the Masters,* is surprising. Clifford Roberts mailed out thousands of letters, many to people he didn't know, with a message from Bobby Jones himself inviting them to join his club. Roberts culled names of prospective members from a list of guests of the Bon Air-Vanderbilt Hotel, from golf clubs, and from other sources, all to little effect. The answer, if any came at all, was usually, "No thanks."

Efforts among acquaintances of Roberts and Jones were more successful, especially at first. The club had sixty-six members by April 1932, pretty good considering that the course wouldn't be ready for play until the following winter. But the club was nearly shut out in trying to find anyone beyond that hardy and enthusiastic band. Two years later, the club had added only ten members, giving it a total of seventy-six at the time of the first Masters.

That simply wasn't going to work economically. The club's bylaws allowed for two thousand members, and Roberts envisioned attracting at least eighteen hundred. His idea was that the low initiation fee and the Jones name would draw people in, and the club would be able to accommodate such a large number because most of them would be out-of-towners.

The plans for the clubhouse, as reported in the *Augusta Chronicle* in October 1931, reflected that vision. The most important thing was the locker room—since this was to be strictly a golf club, a large space for social functions was not required—and the architect was asked to include four hundred lockers, some single and some double.

The clubhouse, which would replace the quaint Fruitland manor house, was designed by Augusta architect Willis Irvin. An artist's rendering showed it to be a whitewashed brick structure with four classic Roman columns adorning the main entrance.

William Marquis of the Olmsted Brothers firm, which was hired for the landscaping of the property, discussed the possibility of saving the old manor house and remodeling it for some use. "For sentimental reasons Augustans would like to see it preserved but Roberts does not care anything about it and says he does not see what practical use could be made of it. I agreed on that. It is not at all modern and would take a lot of money to make it so," Marquis wrote in a report to his firm. "The only possible use I can think of is that it might be entirely remodeled for rooms. If this were done very well and the place was furnished with a lot of nice old furniture, it might be interesting for a certain number of members, but most of them would probably be better satisfied in a modern building with all modern conveniences."

But members would have to learn to live with the old building. A new clubhouse was the first casualty of the club's economic circumstances. The underwriting effort was coming up with (maybe) enough to build the course, but not the additional $100,000 to build a new clubhouse. The club didn't even have the funds to fully renovate the old one until a member paid for it himself in 1941; until then they had to get by with old and in some ways inadequate facilities. It was a small building without much space for a locker room—but that was all right considering how few members had signed up.

In the long run, saving the manor house proved a great, albeit unintentional, move. The club expanded its clubhouse facilities to either side of the old building when better times came after World War II, but it's that central 1854 structure that gives Augusta National its old-fashioned charm. (The small locker room in the original building is used as the Champions' locker room for the Masters, used only by Masters winners.)

"I hope the club never gets foolish and builds a million-dollar clubhouse," Gene Sarazen said on his first trip to Augusta in 1935. They didn't have the funds to be that foolish.

Another plan that never came to fruition was building a second course, sometimes referred to as a "Ladies Course." With a 365-acre property there was plenty of room. There was even space for building lots in addition to two courses. It goes against today's image of Augusta National as pure golf, but originally the idea was to sell part of the property as home sites.

The two uses of the land were intertwined. Olmsted Brothers' Marquis noted that they couldn't map out areas for lots at the start because the club still had to reserve enough land for another eighteen holes. But when it was clear a second course wasn't in the cards, the club turned to selling lots. They had even less success than they did soliciting memberships. Only three were sold, all to the same man, Augusta National member W. Montgomery Harison, who built a large home behind the first green.

Eventually, that property was bought by another member, who sold it back to the club so the house could be torn down in 1977.

The club was officially formed on December 1, 1931, as a corporation with Jones elected president in a meeting held at an Augusta law office. Alfred S. Bourne, who had contributed so heavily to the underwriting, was elected vice president, with the most prominent Augusta members, Fielding Wallace and Charles Phinizy, getting the nod as secretary and treasurer, respectively. The executive committee consisted of Jones, his father Robert P. Jones, Bourne, Roberts, Thomas Barrett, Grantland Rice, and William C. Watt. There was a larger board of governors, too.

Roberts, either at that meeting or later, was named chairman of the executive committee. It was understood that he was running the show day to day—he was the one staying in his office at the club through the whole winter of 1931–32 taking care of all the details. And not just details—he was the one providing the overall vision and making the important decisions. The other members were all pretty busy with their own affairs and relied on Roberts to run the show. The club, in a sense, "belonged" to Jones and Roberts; the idea behind it was Jones's but Roberts was the man who was entrusted with making it happen.

Rice was an important member and one of the first to join. The nation's most well-known sports writer, he not only wrote a syndicated newspaper column but also put together movie shorts (both called "Sportlight"). In what we would consider a conflict of interest today, he would help run the Masters as an important member of the tournament committee and also cover it as a sports writer.

Among the first group of members coming aboard in 1931 was Eugene G. Grace of Bethlehem Steel, along with Bourne of the Singer Sewing Machine family. Others joining a little later included Edward F. Hutton, C. S. Woolworth, Lewis B. Maytag, and Robert W. Woodruff of Coca-Cola. The club was doing well with captains of industry, but there weren't enough of those folks around to reach three digits in membership.

New York was the most fertile ground for finding members—of the thirty members pictured in the 1934 Masters program, sixteen were from New York. It must have been a disappointment to Jones that only two Atlantans signed up, Georgia Power chairman Harry Atkinson right away and Woodruff later. Jones didn't feel that he should play the role of salesman by making a personal pitch to his friends and acquaintances, but he no doubt hoped that some would come on their own.

Roberts tried hard to sign up members from the Southeast, but they weren't biting. Augusta National might have had better luck with local and regional prospective members if it had stayed open all year, but this apparently was never considered.

What about the prestige factor? Jones was certainly revered, and his involvement gave the club some luster. But other than that the club was still an unknown entity. It wasn't until the Masters came along and the course built a reputation as one of the best in the country that the prestige of Augusta National went through the roof. The Jones name by itself wasn't enough to make people join a club they would have to travel to play, or join a second club if they already belonged to one—not during the Depression, anyway.

Clubs were struggling everywhere in the early 1930s. Many had to close because they just couldn't make it. Even established clubs were losing members and trying to survive any way they could. Here's an ad from the March 13, 1932, edition of the *New York Times*:

> "The membership committee of one of America's finest Country Clubs in order to round out their membership have decided to consider a limited number of applicants who will stand strict investigation. Located in New Jersey, convenient to shore resorts. $175 annual dues the only cost. Memberships non-assessable. Initiation fee and investment have been waived."

One gets the feeling that the investigation really wasn't all that strict.

A similar ad in the same edition was for Metropolitan Manor Country Club in Briarcliff Manor, New York. There was no initiation charge or assessments, just $150 annual dues, which included use of the 18-hole course, practice range, miniature course, tennis courts, indoor and outdoor swimming pools, and saddle horses, with no extra fees for any of it.

On the brighter side, one nice touch about the early days of Augusta National was the return of the Berckmans family. Brothers Louis and Allie leaped at the chance to return to the place where they had spent so many years tending to the land when it was a nursery. Sentimentally, they were also returning to where they had grown up—Louis was an infant when the family moved to Augusta and Allie was born on the property.

Louis, seventy-four years old when the club was founded, joined as a member, while sixty-five-year-old Allie was named general manager. They were involved in construction of the golf course in addition to working with Olmsted Brothers in landscaping the rest of the property. By coincidence, Olmsted's Marquis had been given his professional start as a young man when he was hired by the Berckmans to work in Augusta in 1912 in the landscape design part of their business.

Louis remained active in the brothers' newest landscape design company after joining Augusta National, and was the landscape architect of Rockefeller Center in New York City when it was built in the 1930s. At the club, he was responsible for carrying out the idea of naming each hole on the course for a flowering plant or tree, which would be located somewhere on that hole. Some were already there, others had to be transplanted or brought in; Louis was responsible for deciding on the eighteen varieties.

The first public sign of financial distress at Augusta National came with a story in the May 19, 1932, *Chronicle* about water bills. Along with a couple of other requests for relief was one made by Barrett on behalf of Augusta National, asking the waterworks committee of the city council to give the club a flat rate of $100 for all water used between that date and February 15 of next year.

"We have just about been able to balance our budget so far," Barrett told the committee, "and we have no additional memberships in view until next January and February when the winter visitors return to Augusta."

The committee "failed to take any action on the request," the article reported—in other words, it turned him down.

Four days later Augusta National came up in another article about water. The city's waterworks budget had been thrown off by a couple of major items not paid in 1931, including $5,500 from Augusta National for running a line of filtered water out to the property, but now that bill had been paid, albeit a few months late.

Augusta National would be even tardier paying its construction bills. May was a month of reckoning as invoices for the just-completed construction of the course were coming due. But the club was out of money and faced further expenses in the summer with the necessary reconditioning of the manor house into a clubhouse and the care of the grass that had been planted in late May and needed to grow in. Roberts left town for New York on May 21. The club did not expect to be able to sign up any new members until the following winter season, and that meant no ability to pay what it owed to various creditors. All the club could do was issue promissory notes stating that it would pay on February 1, 1933.

We can trace this through a lawsuit filed by the McWane Cast Iron Pipe Supply Company of Birmingham, Alabama, against the Barrett Supply Company of Augusta (run by F. M. Barrett, no relation to Thomas as far as we know). It's a bit complicated because McWane was a sub-sub-contractor, so the $3,000 owed to McWane for the pipes used in the irrigation system was in the form of a note from Augusta National to Claussen-Lawrence Construction Company endorsed to Barrett Supply Company endorsed to McWane. (Claussen-Lawrence and Barrett Supply also held their own notes from Augusta National for $3,000 each. The name at the bottom of the notes was Robt. T. Jones Jr., Pres.)

F. M. Barrett explained the Augusta National situation to McWane, a less sympathetic out-of-town company, in a letter of May 26, 1932. "I would like to advise that there is no question in my mind as to the financial responsibility of this company [Augusta National]. I have been reliably informed that they have already spent in cash over $150,000. They hope to finish the project by the first of December, which is the beginning of our tourist season, and pay off these three $3,000 notes with memberships pledged for the opening of the season. This is one of the largest propositions in the way of golf course, that has ever come into the South, backed by men of enormous wealth, but hard to get in touch with during the summer season as they have all returned to their homes in the North. Please advise us if this arrangement will be satisfactory with you."

It was sort of satisfactory. McWane insisted that the note be passed along with recourse, instead of without recourse, so that if Augusta National failed to pay, Barrett Supply was on the hook. The pipe company also made an arrangement to divide the note into two $1,500 notes and discount one of them at an Augusta bank for cash.

With a golf course ready for play, there was reasonable hope for attracting new members when winter rolled around. But the club would need a lot of new members—probably at least a hundred—in order to satisfy debts that were climbing above $20,000 and pay ongoing expenses. The $60 annual dues collected from existing members wouldn't go very far. Efforts to solicit further underwriting from members were ongoing, but slowing down. Maybe a grand opening would provide the impetus.

The first mention of an opening ceremony came in the *Chronicle* on May 20. The report said that the invitation list for a scheduled December 24 opening included 18,000 prominent people, including governors, golf stars, USGA members, newspapermen, bankers, and others.

On November 3 came word that the opening was postponed until January 12 because the Bon Air-Vanderbilt wasn't scheduled to open until January 9 (not a good sign for the Bon Air-Vanderbilt, by the way, that its season was starting later than usual). No mention was made of the number of invitees, but New York Governor Franklin D. Roosevelt was scheduled to head the list of celebrities—if he won the following week's election, he would be President-elect Roosevelt by then.

Roosevelt did win, but he didn't make it to Augusta. He must have had more important things to do, like planning the New Deal. Ultimately, Roberts arrived at an arrangement for the opening designed to sell the course to prospective members. It would be a three-day affair on January 13, 14, and 15, with prominent citizens traveling to Augusta on a private overnight luxury train from New York (and others arriving from other parts of the country).

This was not the first opening of the course, just the official opening. The first round was played by Bobby Jones back on August 26. Jones had gotten a report on how well the grass had grown in on the fairways and greens and came from Atlanta with his father to check it out. He shot a 72 and pronounced himself quite pleased with the layout.

Augusta National was to be a winter course, so no further activity was recorded until November 7 when Jones visited for one of Rice's "Sportlight" movie shorts to be shot on the new course. It's unclear if Jones played that day or just took some swings for the cameras. Also unclear is how much activity the course received from local members or anyone with connections between August 26 and the informal opening of the course on December 7.

Dr. Ed Bailey, an Augusta pediatrician and the only man to attend each of the first seventy-three Masters tournaments before his death in 2010, recalled getting to play Augusta National before its opening because his neighbor was working on the course and invited him out there (Bailey was sixteen or seventeen at the time).

The course opened for regular play by members and their guests on December 7, christened by a group of about twenty led by Jones. Bobby stayed in town for four days, playing golf on three of them and leading a quail hunting expedition on the other. He shot a 69 in his third round.

Ed Dudley was hired as the course's first professional during that informal opening. Roberts later recalled asking Jones who he wanted for the job. "After some days of reflection, he handed me a paper on which he had written, 'First choice, Ed Dudley; second choice, Macdonald Smith; third choice, Willie Macfarlane,'" Roberts wrote. "I was curious and therefore asked Bob how he arrived at his preferences. He said, 'First of all, I want a gentleman. Next, I feel we should select a pro who likes to teach. And, finally, we want someone who is a good player. You should understand that I do not support the idea that a good teacher can be someone who is not a good striker of the ball. These three professionals qualify on all counts.'"

Dudley auditioned and/or interviewed for the job as he played with Jones, Roberts, Thomas Barrett, and others during the first two days of the informal opening. He didn't fall on his face, so, as Jones's first choice, he was offered the position and accepted. A native of Brunswick, Georgia, Dudley was one of the top twenty players of his day but willing to limit his tournament appearances in favor of club duties. He would retain his position at Wilmington (Delaware) Country Club—later moving to Philadelphia Country Club—in the summer while running the operation and giving lessons at Augusta National in the winter. He demonstrated his playing ability with seven top-ten finishes in the first eight Masters—a tournament he didn't even know would exist at the time he was hired.

Roberts made all the arrangements for the train from New York for the big opening bash. The cost was $100 per person, with everything included—a Pullman berth on the overnight train trip, a room at the

Bon-Air Vanderbilt, all meals, local transportation, and three days of golf. That's not quite the bargain it seems, considering it amounts to about $1,740 in 2012 dollars, but it was a great opportunity for a three-day getaway for the well heeled. Some of the participants were Augusta National members, but for those who weren't it was a rare opportunity to rub shoulders with Bobby Jones.

Accounts differ slightly, but the hundred available spots were either fully subscribed or nearly so, filled by presidents of companies, bankers, lawyers, representatives of the New York Stock Exchange, and other leading lights of the New York business community, with a smattering of Bostonians mixed in.

Several lists had been published, but even the club officials in Augusta weren't quite sure of who had ultimately signed up. "When these men get off the train, we will know who is here," Thomas Barrett told the *Chronicle*.

This group was set to get into Augusta on Friday morning at about 9 AM, but an earlier contingent headed by Grantland Rice arrived on Wednesday on a commercial train, including John Martin, editor of *Time* magazine; B. C. Forbes, editor of *Forbes*; and Paul Patterson, president of the *Baltimore Sun*. Rice's group was there only for the first day of the opening before heading down to Florida on Saturday morning. A group of Atlantans came later in the week and amateur great Francis Ouimet flew down from Boston.

The honored guests were greeted at the club on Friday by "two chipper negro boys in flaming-red uniforms," according to the *Chronicle*, with red-capped Negro caddies waiting to carry their bags. They were also greeted by near freezing weather and rain, an unfortunate turn of events since the temperature had been around 70 earlier in the week. (A group of four from Charlotte, North Carolina, including the mayor, had to take a train instead of a plane when four inches of snow hit that city.)

Many of the hardy guests ventured forth onto the course, but some quit after nine holes due to the weather. Forbes was observed waving his arms around trying to get warm and making comments about the sunny South. "Is there a golf course here?" he asked.

This was in the barbecue tent, one of the main attractions of the day as the collection of mostly Northerners filled and refilled their plates with the wood-fire Southern 'cue. Another way to keep warm was the kegs of corn whiskey at the first and 10th tees provided by the two local members.

"This being during Prohibition good corn was safer and better to drink than scotch or bourbon whiskey available through bootleggers in Georgia," Roberts wrote. "However, some of those present had never drunk corn before, and did not know how strong it was until, let us say, it was too late."

For dessert, there was a special large cake, with figures of golfers on top, presented by a local bakery.

Most of the men came by themselves, but a few brought their wives. "There are no ladies on this trip," Mrs. Charles Sabin joked to a *Chronicle* reporter as she was chatting with other wives in the clubhouse. "You see many of the men told their wives there would be no wives on the trip and left them at home as golf widows while they are down here.

"But some of the wives sneaked off and joined the party. But we are good sports and don't want the wives back North to know we are having the time of our lives in the South."

Asked to comment on the occasion, Roberts replied, "Do you mean the course or the weather? You can't print what I think about the weather, but the entire affair is splendid. All we can ask for."

Roberts and others have written of a very dramatic moment at a meeting of Augusta National members held at the Bon Air-Vanderbilt Friday evening. Just when Jones was about to make his opening remarks, Rice stood up and said that he had been a member of promising new clubs that had failed because they held too many meetings. He proposed that Jones and Roberts be allowed to run things as they saw fit, without committees or meetings getting in the way, and everyone agreed.

If this even happened, it would hardly have caused a ripple. The club had already been in existence for more than a year, and that's exactly how it was already being run; Roberts making all of the decisions, in consultation with Jones when he felt it necessary. No one seemed to have a problem with that. So letting the founding duo run the club as they saw fit was merely maintaining the status quo.

Jones didn't even play on the first day of the opening because he spent his time greeting and conversing with people. On Sunday, though, he shot a 69, placing an exclamation point on the festivities.

The train headed north on Sunday evening, full of wealthy men with stories to tell. But was it full of men seriously considering joining Augusta National Golf Club? No.

It had been a nice party and everything, but joining a new golf club that was a full day's train ride away just wasn't practical in these times even for company bigwigs. According to Owen only one member of the party ended up joining the club. The opening had been a smash, but unsuccessful in fulfilling its main purpose. Nor did Rice's "Sportlight" movie short seem to bring any potential new members knocking on the door.

As a result, the club's financial crisis deepened. The people knocking on the door were creditors, and they included Olmsted Brothers and MacKenzie. The doctor had halved his design fee from $10,000 to $5,000 a year earlier, but had been paid only $2,000, an amount that might not have even covered his expenses. In financial straits himself, MacKenzie wrote a series of pleading letters to Roberts asking for his money, throwing in touches of humor such as, "I have been reduced to playing golf with four clubs and a Woolworth ball." Lack of funds was undoubtedly the reason MacKenzie didn't make the cross-country trip to Augusta for the course opening.

All Roberts could manage was to send MacKenzie a couple of notes with a value of $1,000 each, which he might be able to dispose of at a discount, though Roberts warned him not to try to discount them in Augusta.

Some of the creditors held notes that were supposed to be paid on February 1, 1933, at 6 percent interest. Those notes for construction costs billed in 1932 remained unpaid past that due date.

If ever there were a time when you could play Augusta National, this was it. The club wasn't turning anyone down, as guest fees were the only way they were managing to meet payroll every week. On March 2, the *Chronicle* reported that sixty golfers played the course the previous day. In April, the club played host to a golf outing for the American Bankers Association convention being held in Augusta. And in May it hosted the annual tournament of the Augusta Cotton Exchange.

This was a trickle that allowed the club to pay its employees, but no one else.

Even this trickle had figuratively been frozen for much of February by frigid weather that led Roberts to lament, "We might just as well be in Canada as far as playing golf is concerned." Apparently, Augusta's idea of a winter golf destination was a place that gave you a real touch of winter.

March brought better weather but not better prospects, with Roberts writing that he didn't see a chance of securing "even a single membership check" now that the season was nearing its close, according to *The Making of the Masters*.

So, Roberts wrote a letter on March 20, 1933, addressed to the creditors of Augusta National Golf Club. He stated that the club was "embarrassed" by debts amounting to about $31,000, that the "small group of sportsmen" that advanced $120,000 couldn't contribute any more, and that President Robert T. Jones Jr. had voluntarily contributed $10,000 but couldn't be asked to do more. (It's legitimate to wonder why he didn't put in more money, considering the enormous sum he received from Warner Brothers.)

"For this reason, we are forced to say to you that the club can not now pay the sum that is due to you," Roberts wrote. "The Augusta National is obligated on a sixty thousand ($60,000) dollar mortgage which covers the golf course, club house, and grounds. If trouble is made by any owner of current obligations, this mortgage will be foreclosed, the enterprise wrecked, and the sponsorship of Mr. Jones will be lost. In the interest of all concerned, we propose to the creditors a Stand-Still-Agreement ending April 15, 1934."

"Practically all" of the Augusta creditors went along with the extension plan, F. M. Barrett wrote in a March 30 letter to the skeptics at Birmingham's McWane Cast Iron Pipe Supply Company.

The club's plans have been upset to such an extent, he wrote, that "the only thing left for them to do will be for their creditors to extend further time as bankruptcy or receivership would mean an entire loss to every creditor. . . . They are very hopeful that conditions will be better and that they will be able to pay their outstanding indebtedness at the close of their next season."

Well, that's what they said last year, too. But the creditors had little choice but to wait and hope things improved. You can't draw blood from a stone. The Augusta city council went along, too. It agreed in May to turn an outstanding water bill of $2,282.82 into a note payable the following February 1, with Augusta National agreeing to pay its ongoing water bills until then in cash.

As for Roberts and Jones, their primary thought must have been one that Roberts expressed later in his book: "Had we known [when starting the club] that [the Depression] was to become a lot worse, and not end until a world war came along, I am very certain that we would have called off the project."

# 5

# THE IDEA/
# THE MASTERS IS HATCHED

---

**T**HERE WAS A STRONG United States Golf Association presence at Augusta National's opening party. This was only natural since Jones had won four U.S. Opens and five U.S. Amateurs run by the organization and naturally was a favorite of the USGA brass. What's more, as golfers, they were curious to see the course that had sprung from the minds of Jones and Alister MacKenzie.

George Herbert Walker, former USGA president (and grandfather of future President George H. W. Bush); vice president John G. Jackson; secretary Archie M. Reid; and treasurer Charles H. Sabin (an Augusta National member) were all on hand. Jones played on Saturday with Walker, Jackson, and Reid, who came away very impressed with the course.

"I think that something quite new has been introduced by Bobby," Jackson told William D. Richardson of the *New York Times*. "His use of mounds through the fairway and around the greens brings about an effect similar to the dunes at St. Andrews and on other seaside courses in the old country.

"This use of mounds instead of traps, as is the general practice here, carries out the same general effect and will result in quite a saving in upkeep. I see no reason why first-class golf courses cannot be built along these lines and maintained at much less cost."

Reid also enthused about the layout.

"It is a great golf course," he said. "What I liked particularly about it was the type of greens Bobby has built. They are like St. Andrews, big rolling greens with interesting contours and almost no trapping. In order to be reasonably certain of getting down in two putts you've got to watch your step carefully. You've got to come into the hole the correct way or else you are going to find yourself taking an extra putt to get down."

A month later, in February, Walker's son-in-law, Prescott Bush, visited Augusta National at Roberts's invitation. Bush was the president of the USGA's tournament committee, and while in Augusta he discussed the possibility of the Jones/MacKenzie creation hosting the 1934 U.S. Open (the USGA in those days didn't name its Open sites several years ahead of time as it does now).

The prospect delighted Jones. As a Southerner, he would have been proud for his course and club to be the first in that part of the country to host a U.S. Open.

Bush told Roberts that the matter would be discussed by the USGA's executive committee. But as much as the USGA people liked the course, that discussion centered on a number of problems. The U.S. Open was played in June. Augusta National wasn't open at that time of year, and even if it changed its policy to stay open through early June to accommodate the championship it might be oppressively hot.

Most likely, the event would have to be held in March or early April. But that created problems with sectional qualifying, as courses in the Northeast and Upper Midwest wouldn't be ready for play. The USGA was highly skeptical of being able to hold an Open at that time of year.

What's more, the U.S. Open in those days didn't stray from major population centers, since smaller cities or resort areas wouldn't be able to draw enough spectators to create much in the way of gate receipts. With a population of about sixty thousand, Augusta wasn't really big enough.

In April, USGA president Herbert Jaques wrote Roberts saying that "whereas we are all favorably inclined to this move in the near future, we do not think it is practical to attempt in 1934."

Keeping the option open for the future probably meant that the USGA was willing to consider holding the Open in March or April, but needed more time to consider how to make it work. Or perhaps they felt that June in Augusta might be acceptable after all, or that they could meet halfway and hold it in May.

But, on his end, Roberts was beginning to formulate his own idea. One reason he was excited about the possibility of an Open was the publicity it would generate for the club—publicity that could lead to new members. If there was any way out of the hole Augusta National found itself in, this was it.

Immediate help was needed. So instead of waiting on the U.S. Open in a future year, why shouldn't Augusta National hold its own tournament in 1934? And instead of an occasional U.S. Open, why not a tournament every year? Thus, the Masters was born primarily as a way of drumming up membership for a struggling new club.

True, a tournament staged by the club wouldn't have the prestige of a national championship. But there was a way that it could have as much *impact* as a U.S. Open—it could boast of Bobby Jones as a competitor.

Would Jones agree to come out of retirement to play in a tournament? There were a few reasons he might.

First, it wasn't a championship of anything. There's no way Jones would play in a U.S. Open. That would be a return to the competitive grind he had left behind and clearly never wanted to join again. But he might play in a more low-key tournament.

Jones wanted his club to be successful. At this point, he just wanted his club to survive. He also wanted to showcase the golf course he and MacKenzie had created. The tournament was a means to those ends. A tournament *without* Jones might not be enough to accomplish those goals; a tournament *with* Jones might. It would attract much more media attention and bigger headlines nationwide. From a bottom-line perspective, it would mean much higher gate receipts.

He would enjoy getting together with old acquaintances among the top amateur and professional players of the day. And more of them might be drawn to play if Jones were in the field.

Jones must have had *some* competitive juices remaining. The prospect of seeing how he stacked up against a field of strong players probably had some appeal, as long as it was in a relatively low-key environment.

The one thing that probably made Jones hesitate was that he didn't want this to become a Return of Bobby Jones story that would turn the event into a pressure cooker for him. In the back of his mind, he must have known that's exactly what would happen—and it did. But the other points were too persuasive. If that's the way it had to be, Jones would just have to deal with it. He was essentially painted into a corner.

Roberts used his powers of persuasion to get Jones to agree to play. He later wrote that "the final argument that persuaded Bob to agree to play, or so he said, was one I advanced, to the effect that he simply could not invite his friends to play on his course and then decline to play with them."

Perhaps that's true—but more likely the cold, hard financial realities were the biggest factor. Jones in the field meant a better chance for the club to make money, either directly through selling tickets or indirectly through publicity that would help to draw members.

But financial realities also threw up a potential roadblock to staging a tournament. It costs money to run an event like that. A purse of at least $5,000 would have to be paid to the professionals. Scoreboards and perhaps tents would have to be erected, facilities would need to be provided for the press, tickets would have to be printed, personnel would be required to help run the event. And Roberts and Jones felt some work needed to be put into the young course to bring it into top condition. Where would all of that come from when the club was already behind on its bills?

Roberts had an answer: Ask the City of Augusta for cash.

It wasn't as brazen a request as it might seem. Augusta prided itself as being a winter golf destination. A tournament at Augusta National featuring Bobby Jones could be expected to draw many spectators from out of town, who would patronize hotels and pump money into the city. What's more, the publicity generated by a tournament that would be ballyhooed in the newspapers as Jones's return to action would serve as a kind of advertising for Augusta and potentially draw more winter visitors.

Indeed, during the 1930s—the days well before corporate sponsorship—most events on the pro tour were sponsored by chambers of commerce or similar organizations in cities or resort areas seeking to increase the business or tourist profile of their location. The logic was the same for the City of Augusta, except that it wouldn't be *running* the tournament only providing some of the funding.

Roberts decided to ask the city council for $10,000. The request was made at a council meeting on August 8, 1933, by club secretary Fielding Wallace. The task might have fallen to Wallace because it came during the summer when Roberts was in New York, but in any case it was probably viewed as better that the request should come from an Augustan.

Here's how Wallace made his case.

- The tournament would bring 20,000 people to Augusta for the week. Projecting an average of $50 per person, they would account for $1 million in spending. The estimate of 20,000 came from Grantland Rice. It's a figure that could only have been drawn out of thin air and it bore no relation to reality, as we shall see. But Rice was a foremost authority on sports, so his words carried some weight.
- The Savannah River and tourists are the only things that can make Augusta a big city, and the tourist business is recognized as the biggest in the world. This tied in with Augusta's ambitions, which were very high, as espoused in the *Chronicle*. Just two weeks earlier, the newspaper had projected in an editorial that the creation of a nine-foot channel in the Savannah would turn Augusta into a great inland port that would be "the metropolis of the Southeast," with a population that would quadruple to a quarter million in twenty-five years. It also said, "We are ambitious to become the nation's premier resort city, and the winter golf capital of the world, which is certain to happen." The proposal of a major golf tournament fed right into those dreams.
- Bobby Jones has linked his reputation with Augusta because he saw the greatest opportunity there for an ideal golf center in his native state, and his name has already attracted some of

the greatest business figures in the country as evidenced by the course opening in January.

- It will be an elite tournament, limited to thirty of the leading golfers in the world, as chosen by a committee of sports writers. Jones has agreed to reenter competition for this tournament only.

- Not only would the tournament fill hotels, it would bring thousands of prospective buyers of winter homes.

- The newspaper coverage of the tournament across the country would secure greater publicity for the city than could be bought at any price.

The proposal was not without opposition. Councilman C. C. Murphey objected, saying that a tournament would benefit only a few and not the rank and file of the city. Councilman Harry L. Woodward said that such an appropriation would be "foolish" considering the current state of the city's finances.

Legal questions were raised and addressed by the city's attorney. Augusta National was outside the city limits in an unincorporated part of Richmond County and the council was not allowed to make an appropriation "to any interest unless directly associated with the municipality." However, the attorney ruled that it *would* be legal for the city to appropriate $10,000 for municipal advertising and allot the sum to Augusta National for promotion of the tournament. The resort hotels were inside city limits in an area on a hill west of downtown called Summerville that had been annexed in 1911, so most of the economic benefits would be felt in the city. Augusta National was just outside the city line.

Asked if the $10,000 represented the total cost of putting on the tournament, Wallace replied that the total would be in the neighborhood of $50,000. He was not asked for details on that estimate, which must have included a lot of course work, and in any case might have been exaggerated to make it appear that the club was doing its share, too, and not relying solely on the city. Wallace did say that the club would like to raise the tournament purse above the proposed $5,000 if possible. (The purse stayed at $5,000, not just for 1934 but all the way through 1942.)

A vote was held on whether to refer the appropriation to the finance committee, which would determine if the money could be raised. Essentially a vote on the appropriation itself, the motion passed eight to two.

Augusta National could look forward to support from city hall in the future, too. Thomas Barrett, who helped Roberts find and secure the Fruitland property, had won the Democratic primary for mayor a month earlier, assuring that he would become the city's next chief executive.

In an editorial a day after the report of the meeting, the *Chronicle* called the proposed tournament "the greatest golf event in the world's history." What's more, "The entire community, once it realizes what this golf event is going to mean for the development of this city as a winter resort, and with huge sums of money expended here every year that is now going to Pinehurst, Miami, Palm Beach, and other places will applaud City Council for its splendid attitude, and we have no hesitancy in predicting that the finance committee will probably vote this appropriation."

The finance committee did approve—and the Masters was on its way.

On August 23, the tournament was announced to the world in Rice's "Sportlight" column, playing up the Jones-returns-to-competition angle.

"After nearly four years retirement from competitive golf, Bobby Jones, the ex-mandarin of wood and iron, will lug his war clubs back into action in one of the big tournaments of golf," read the lead.

Instead of a committee of sports writers inviting thirty players, Rice now had it as a committee of the club inviting fifty pros and ten amateurs. Jones was quoted as agreeing to play "if I happen to be one of the fifty or sixty golfers named by the committee. I've been out of action so long I may not belong in this group."

There was no way of avoiding it—even his friend Rice painted the competition as a test of whether Jones was still the best in the game even after four years of retirement.

"It will be the natural desire of all the leading professionals to prove that they have left the old Jones banner fluttering behind the pack," Rice wrote. "You can gamble that Jones will be just as keen to prove that he can still swing a golf club with the same old punch and skill."

Some controversy still remained about the city funding. Councilman Woodward objected in September when $2,800 was paid to Augusta National out of what was supposed to be a nurses home furnishing fund. Mayor W. D. Jennings responded that the matter was handled properly and that it merely amounted to a loan from the fund that would soon be repaid.

Augusta National's Wallace had made a request for $3,000 of the appropriated $10,000 to be given right away in order to make improvements to the course.

"Personally, I am convinced that the tournament is to prove an excellent thing for Augusta and I think also that it is up to the city to help with it," the mayor said. "If, then, we are going to have the tournament, we should put the golf course in shape for play. Work like that has to be done months before the course is to be used."

Woodward said that he had spoken with laborers at the course who said the $2,800 was to be used to pay them. "I have also been told that the tournament will not cost near the amount they have said they would need," the councilman added.

Given the financial affairs of the club, Woodward was probably right about how the money was used. He was also probably right that running the tournament wouldn't cost $50,000.

Be that as it may, the decision had already been made to give the club $10,000. And all things considered, it was a justifiable decision.

The club chose March 22 to 25 as the dates of the tournament, near the end of Augusta's resort season, and informed the PGA of their intentions so they could be put on the schedule. It fit nicely between tournaments in Charleston and Pinehurst, and in October was announced as part of the PGA Tour's winter tour schedule.

In December, Rice came to town and found himself as the interview subject instead of the interviewer. Asked about the prospects for the Augusta tournament, he said it "will eventually equal the National Open [U.S. Open] in importance."

His statement would prove to be more than wishful thinking.

# 6

# THE TOUR/GROWTH IN HARD TIMES

O NE MIGHT THINK THAT the Depression would have been a time of decline for the pro tour. Instead, it was a time of expansion.

What was an informal winter tour in the 1920s had become a year-round tour by 1935, with a manager appointed by the PGA to line up dates and run the show, plenty of places willing to put up money to host a golf tournament and bring publicity to their city or resort, and some financial backing from golf-equipment manufacturers.

Purses of individual tournaments declined in some places after 1929, especially those that had put up big bucks in the late 1920s. But the total purse available on tour increased because there were more events.

The number of players on the tour increased, too. Some were driven there because there were fewer club jobs to be had because of the Depression. A number of clubs folded when hard economic times hit, leaving their pros out on the street. Other clubs survived but had to cut an assistant pro from their staff.

Of course, the tour was a hard way to make a living. In 1934, the leading money winner, Paul Runyan, collected $6,768, the tenth leading money winner $3,709, and the 20th earned $1,973. In 1935, the first year with a full summer schedule instead of a partial one, those numbers were $9,543 (the leader was Johnny Revolta), $3,380, and $2,266. Tournament purses in 1935 ranged from $3,000 to $10,000, with between fourteen and twenty players getting paid each week.

"There was so little money that we didn't take ourselves too seriously," Runyan recalled to writer Al Barkow for the book *Gettin' to the Dance Floor.* "We fought like cats and dogs for the titles, but the money didn't seem to make that much difference. So there were a lot of antics, fun, camaraderie."

The group traveling around together was fairly small, a far cry from the couple hundred players who populate the tour today. Tournament players ran the gamut from a small core who could play the entire tour, a couple of stars in any given year who could skip a lot of tournaments and play on lucrative exhibition tours instead, and pros with club jobs that let them off for varying amounts of time. Some played the whole winter tour but couldn't get off in the summer; others were let off by their clubs to play in some of the more prestigious summer events. Some played the Florida and Southeast portions of the winter tour but didn't go west; others played in California and Arizona but didn't go east.

In 1935, only thirteen pros played more than seventy rounds, which could be considered a full schedule, and only seven more played between fifty and seventy. The rest were part-timers.

The better players had deals with equipment companies that paid $3,000 or so annually, helping to cover travel expenses. A lucky few represented clubs that didn't require very much of their presence. Some, like Runyan, had their expenses paid by members at their clubs, in his case Metropolis Country Club in New York, generally with an agreement to share the profits.

Some drove from tournament to tournament by car, which was not a very comfortable way to go in the 1930s. Many took the train. Those who traveled by rail needed transportation once they got to the tournament city. That's why PGA tournament bureau manager Bob Harlow's guidelines for local tournament committees stated that providing transportation was necessary. "In case your location is such that provision will have to be made for transporting contestants, it has been found useful to utilize busses operating from a central point on regular schedule. If you are so situated that there will be considerable taxicab traffic, the most satisfactory arrangement is to make arrangement with a taxicab company for a flat rate."

Nothing in there about courtesy cars!

In an introduction to the PGA guidelines, Harlow explained the rationale for holding a tournament.

"It is not possible for every community to have a 'Rose Bowl' football game, but it is quite possible for a large number of communities to hold an annual open golf championship. These events are often sponsored by Junior Chambers of Commerce, and these active organizations of the younger business men put their energy and effort behind open golf tournaments and promote them in such a manner as to bring the most favorable reactions. . . . As a feature for winter and summer resorts, open golf tournaments have been recognized for many years."

The idea was that your city appearing in the dateline of tournament reports carried in newspapers across the country would plant a seed in readers' minds that Pinehurst or St. Petersburg or Phoenix or wherever would be a nice place to go on their next vacation.

Harlow pointed out that tournaments in a major population center could be self supporting through ticket sales and other sources of income, thus explaining how financially strapped cities could none-theless hold golf events. Tournaments in resort areas might lose money, but that could be written off as advertising. In this context, the city of Augusta giving money to the Masters was not unusual.

Finding funds wasn't always easy, though. In 1934, *PGA Magazine* reported that the PGA was having difficulty putting together the Florida schedule. "Many Florida municipalities are having trouble keeping their schools open and city budgets which formerly contained appropriations for the promotion of recreations and other features have been cut to the bone." A golf tournament did seem rather frivolous in comparison.

To help in such situations, Harlow had persuaded the Golf Ball and Golf Club Manufacturers Association from 1931 onward to contribute a fund to the PGA that could be used to supplement purses.

The tournament manager was a relatively new position, first established in the season of 1929–30 to impose some order on a chaotic situation in which tournament sponsors scheduled their events on whatever dates they wished with little coordination. It was more orderly by the mid-1930s, but it was still a scramble. Often, the schedule wouldn't fall into place until a month or two before the winter tour or summer tour started.

Problems would emerge, such as in 1935 when no sponsors for Texas events could be found. However, with new tournaments on the West Coast and Florida, there was no resulting gap in the schedule. In fact, there were so many smallish tournaments popping up that over-crowding of the schedule was becoming a problem. The watchword from now on, Harlow said in the fall of 1934, was "fewer and better tournaments."

With 36-hole finales the rule, it took only three days to complete a tournament. During particularly busy parts of the schedule, three tournaments could be packed into a two-week span.

Two roles of the tournament manager were to formalize the way tournaments were run and to generate publicity. These came together in the matter of tournament pairings. Previously, players often made their own pairings and tee times, but now they were arranged by Harlow and the tournament committee. This was not only a more professional way to handle things, it enabled Harlow to release the pairings to the local newspaper in advance.

Players sometimes complained about their pairings or times—and that's not the only problem that Harlow had with his charges. Behavior became such an issue that a code of conduct was put in place in 1934.

The code led off with an admonition that one would not think necessary: "Players participating in any sort of competition must observe the rules for that particular event and the etiquette of golf."

Next came the matter of committing to tournaments. "Players should enter events as early as possible so their names can be used in helping to advertise the events and to make matters easier for the local committees. Players should be on time and in instances where they have entered an event and have to withdraw, they should notify the committee."

Grumbling about the pairings made by the tournament committee led to this one: "Players should not request special starting times or partners."

Here's a surprising one. Some top players had taken to bringing their own caddies with them from event to event. Rank-and-file members complained that it put them at a disadvantage. So the code stated, "Players must not employ 'traveling caddies.' This is merely taking advantage of the field. Players must take local caddies as provided by the local clubs."

Finally, "Players should not criticize courses on which tournaments are played."

The last problem continued to bother the PGA even after the Code of Conduct was put in place.

"The Tournament Committee should start a campaign to make the players refrain from making uncalled for cracks in locker rooms to club members about the course, etc. They should likewise be more considerate about playing practice shots from fairways or club house lawns and such," Harlow wrote in 1935. "These are two things you can pass rules about all night long but the only way to stop them will be by example and by getting the big boys in the game to talk about these things and to keep the ears and eyes open and speak a word whenever they hear or see boys talking out of turn or mutilating spots that they should protect."

The Code of Conduct gave the PGA president the power, after an investigation by the tournament committee, to bar players from competition for various periods of time. It was really more of an honor code, since it was unlikely suspensions would be handed out except for serious violations.

Harlow's comment implies that the "big boys" weren't the problem when it came to etiquette (though they were the target of the admonition to enter tournaments early enough to allow for publicity). Who were the big boys?

From the viewpoint of the twenty-first century, the early to middle 1930s were an era lacking in "big boys." Bobby Jones and Walter Hagen dominated golf in the 1920s, but Jones's retirement and Hagen's age-induced decline (he was born in 1892) left a void that wasn't completely filled until the emergence of Byron Nelson, Sam Snead, and Ben Hogan in the late 1930s.

Contemporaries didn't quite see it that way. There was Gene Sarazen—not quite as huge a figure as Jones or Hagen had been but a star nonetheless. And it seemed like there was always a candidate to be the "next Bobby Jones," even if none of them panned out in the long run.

First came Horton Smith, who charged out of the blocks at the start of his career with twelve wins in 1929–30. After Sarazen reasserted himself by winning the U.S. and British Opens—a Jones-like feat—in 1932, the next youngster to take center stage was Runyan, who reeled off fifteen wins in 1933–34. And in 1935 Henry Picard and Johnny Revolta became big names with five wins apiece. They didn't have the staying power of Jones and Hagen, or, later, Snead, Hogan, and Nelson, but there were always a couple of players on which the tour could hang its hat at any given time.

But it was the tour as a whole that impressed observers in the mid-1930s. When Jones returned to competition at the 1934 Masters, it was frequently pointed out that the competition was much tougher than when he had retired, even though just four years had passed.

This impression arose in part because of the much lower scoring. Jones used to talk about the battle with Old Man Par, but by the 1930s pros were regularly kicking Old Man Par around. Scores in the 270s for four rounds, previously unheard of, were now not uncommon.

A big reason for the improved scoring was the switch to steel shafts, which occurred over the course of the late 1920s and early 1930s. Sports writers were aware of this, of course, but they were still dazzled by the numbers.

They also were impressed with the depth of the tour. A superstar like Jones or Hagen would no longer have easy pickings, because the tour had strength in numbers. You might beat Players A, B, C, D, and E, which a few years earlier would have been enough to win the tournament, but now Player F might have a hot week and beat you.

Finally, there was the idea that the expansion in the number of tournaments had resulted in a corps of players whose games had been tempered by constant competition.

"Because of the abundant opportunity for competition under fire, our players have developed competitive golfing temperaments which are unequaled," Harlow wrote. "Many professional golfers in Great Britain are as skillful hitters of the ball as the Americans, but they lack the wide tournament experience of our men. So while the sponsors of open tournament golf in all sections of America have had their own purpose for promoting these events, they have each contributed a share toward making American professional golf outstanding."

A group of young players, all twenty-six or younger, made a favorable impression on Atlanta golf writer O. B. Keeler when he had a chance to see them in 1934. About Runyan, Ky Laffoon, Revolta, Dick Metz, and Picard, he wrote that he was not only impressed with their golf, they were "Great kids—clean-cut, well mannered, modest, and always sportsmen. The good old game of golf, so it appears to me, is rather getting up in the world."

Coming from a man best known for chronicling Jones's feats, this was a stamp of approval for the next generation—an indication that Jones's retirement didn't leave an unfillable void. (One area where Jones's absence really did hurt was at the U.S. Open, where gate receipts dropped dramatically; it didn't affect other tour events, because Jones hadn't played them.)

PGA president George Jacobus felt the same way about the youngsters on tour.

"These chaps are in perfect physical condition; train as vigorously as oarsmen," he said. "They do not drink 'hard stuff,' keep late hours, or play the cabaret circuit. These mentally fresh, nervously stable youngsters eat, sleep, and think golf. Tournament golf, ever a jealous mistress, has become a highly specialized science."

Throughout 1933 and 1934, the hottest player by far was twenty-five-year-old Runyan. He was an unlikely star. At five-foot-seven, 125 pounds, Runyan was one of the shortest hitters on tour and had an ungraceful swing, swaying off the ball on the backswing and then lunging through. But he was accurate with his fairway wood and long iron approach shots and uncanny with his short game and putting.

George Trevor said he had the best short-game feel of any player since 1915 U.S. Open champion Jerry Travers.

"Through necessity, I began my lifelong devotion to the short game," Runyan later wrote, "the searching for shortcuts that would somehow let me compete, and hopefully excel, in a world of stronger players."

The greatest good fortune of Runyan's life was that he grew up on a farm across from Hot Springs Country Club in Little Rock, Arkansas. He took to the game immediately, especially when he saw that he could make more money as a young caddie than his father could on the farm.

His father thought golf was frivolous and at first punished Paul for going to the golf course. "I finally looked him in the eye and said, 'Dad, you can whip me if you want, but it won't do you any good, because I'm going over to the golf course, and I'm going to become a golf professional.'" The objections ceased when Runyan's father realized that Paul was bringing home $45 a week in addition to his own spending money. But he never in his life saw Paul play golf—not a single hole.

Runyan's enthusiasm and desire were so great that in almost no time he moved up from the caddie yard to become an apprentice to pro Jimmy Norton, and he dropped out of school after the eighth grade. Hot Springs was a big operation, a resort with three courses. There was much work for an apprentice to do from cleaning and repairing clubs to shagging balls on the range, and, eventually, giving lessons himself, even as a teenager. Runyan got to rub shoulders with, and sometimes play with, celebrity athletes such as Babe Ruth, Gene Tunney, Walter Johnson, and Goose Goslin—not to mention the Chicago gangsters who wintered at Hot Springs.

Runyan was lucky that he escaped the caddie yard so quickly, for caddies weren't allowed to play the course (though he used to sneak on and play five holes in the morning on his way to school). So he was able to work on his game to the point where he won the Arkansas Open just before his seventeenth birthday. That got him an offer to be the professional at Concordia Country Club in Little Rock.

In contrast to the hustle and bustle of Hot Springs, Concordia was a small club where the members played mostly on Wednesday afternoons and Sundays. Runyan had plenty of time to practice, and that's where he developed his extraordinary short game.

Concordia's members financed their young pro to play the West Coast portion of the winter tour in 1929 and again in 1930. The ambitious Runyan used the second swing to try to meet a pro who could give him an assistant job in the New York or Chicago areas—and he found one in Craig Wood.

Wood had broken through as a tour player two years earlier. Runyan and Wood made for an odd couple—Wood was six-foot-one, weighed more than 200 pounds, and was one of the game's longest hitters—but a good team. Wood had been hired mainly because of his reputation as a player, but he needed somebody to help him run his shop at Forest Hill Field Club in New Jersey and Runyan had a good head for business.

"He had no bookkeeping at all. He didn't keep inventories," Runyan remembered in a USGA oral history interview. So Runyan, still just twenty-one years old, set up the bookkeeping system he had learned at Hot Springs.

Runyan was making a reputation as a player, too. On the way east to start the Forest Hill job he detoured to North Carolina and won the North and South Open, a prestigious event on the tour. He added the New Jersey Open title in the summer of 1930.

Wood left for another New Jersey club, Deal Country Club, in 1931 and Runyan was set to take over as head pro at Forest Hill when he had a better offer from Metropolis Country Club in White Plains, New York. "I was offered the head job there by Mr. Gerald Rosenberger,"

Runyan recalled. "One night he had me and my wife come to his house in New York, on Park Avenue, for an interview with the club board. Everyone was there in black tie—they had a dinner—and I was very impressed. . . . It was a great break, because Metropolis was the highest-grade establishment I ever worked at."

Runyan beat Sarazen to win the Metropolitan PGA that summer and also won the Westchester Open. Despite Runyan's small stature and less-than-classic swing, Rosenberger saw that he had the potential to be a special player so he organized a group of his fellow members to back Paul on the winter tour of 1931–32. It was a good move, as Runyan's winnings exceeded his expenses each year. And it was even better for Paul, as the members didn't take their share of the profits and even gave him a bonus his first year.

Of course, it was good publicity to have your pro doing well on tour. And during the Depression it was good business because it could make the difference in attracting new members and keeping the ones you had. Plus, they genuinely liked Runyan.

Runyan was a world-beater on the 1933–34 winter tour, with seven individual victories and two team wins. He led in money earnings for the calendar years 1933 and 1934, the latter being the first year that the PGA tallied money that way instead of just counting winter tour earnings. He had nine wins in 1933 and six in 1934.

"He is the nearest approach to a perfect scoring machine that has developed since Bobby Jones," Joseph Glass wrote in *Literary Digest* in 1934.

Horton Smith was one of Runyan's best friends on tour, and he gave this analysis of what made Paul so good.

"His marvelous temperament, his ambition to do his job very thoroughly, and his excellent short game make him stand out head and shoulders above the rest of the boys in the last three months of play," Smith said at the end of the 1934 winter tour.

Beyond that, Smith noted that Runyan had a unique feel that extended beyond his short game. "I think Paul has the most sensitive pair of hands in the golf business. He can start his swing and know by the initial feel that something is wrong and can correct it before the ball seems to get away. Few of the rest of us, once a swing is underway, can do a thing about it, but Paul has the power to control his shots at all times."

Runyan felt that he even had luck on his side—but it wasn't really luck, it was sound course management.

"My theory is that ninety percent of all luck is a question of good or bad judgment," he said. "I always try to create my good luck by good judgment."

Runyan didn't possess the showmanship of Hagen or the graceful swing and national championship record of Jones. He wasn't carrying the tour on his frail shoulders, but he didn't have to. It was a team effort in the 1930s, and the tour was getting along fine with what it had.

# 7

# 1934 PRE-MASTERS/THE BUILD-UP

**P**LANS FOR THE FIRST Masters were very fluid in the months leading up to the tournament.

Fielding Wallace's presentation to the city council indicated that there would be only thirty players in the field. A few weeks later, Grantland Rice wrote that there would be fifty or sixty. Ultimately, more than ninety were invited and seventy-two players competed.

While one reason for the original low number was to sell the tournament as a super elite event, another was that club members at first didn't want to be deprived of playing their course during the season. The thought was that with a very small field, members could play the course in the morning with tournament tee times in the afternoon.

The PGA couldn't have been too fond of this idea. In any case, the club quickly dropped it and began focusing on the spectator experience rather than the members' desires. With a larger field, there could be marquee pairings sent out in both the morning and afternoon, enabling the fans to see more than one twosome. Also, special events could be held each morning as an enhancement for the fans.

Those included a putting contest on Thursday, an iron contest on Friday, and a longest drive contest on Saturday, in addition to an alternate-shot competition on Wednesday, the last practice day. Sunday would be reserved for the final round, and that was a story in itself.

Nearly all 72-hole stroke-play tournaments in that era were conducted over the course of three days, with 36 holes played on the final day. They typically ended on a Saturday, though some events were even held in the middle of the week. Jones had the idea to spread the tournament over four days, with no double rounds, in order to leave room for the special events. Fortunately, there were no blue laws in Augusta preventing sporting events on Sundays.

Playing in four days meant an extra day of gate receipts, which undoubtedly appealed to Clifford Roberts. He also liked it because he felt it was fairer for players who were "unable to do their best scoring if forced to play 36 holes in one day."

(The Masters wasn't the first tournament to use this format, but it was among the first. The Agua Caliente Open, a tour event in Mexico, was a 72-hole event already being played in four days before 1934.)

A very basic decision that engendered some internal debate was the name of the tournament. Roberts intended to call it the Masters, but Jones thought that immodest. Jones won a very limited victory in that argument. At his insistence, the tournament's official name was the Augusta National Invitation Tournament. However, Roberts and Wallace had already let the cat out of the bag by referring to the tournament as the Masters before that decision was made.

The *Augusta Chronicle* started calling it the Masters from the time the idea of the tournament was first broached, and never stopped calling it that. In all the hundreds of articles about the tournament by

*Chronicle* writers, only one called it the Augusta National Invitation Tournament.

There were a lot of variations on the name. The PGA's schedule of 1933–34 winter tournaments listed it as the Augusta National Open. It was sometimes called the Masters Open, and even appeared in newspapers on occasion as the Bobby Jones Tournament. Most importantly, the Associated Press and United Press wire services called it the Masters (more precisely, they called it the Masters Invitation tournament and the Masters' Invitation Golf Tournament, respectively.)

Augusta National member Rice in an August 1933 article called it "an open invitation tournament to be presented by Augusta National" but as the tournament got closer he was calling it the Masters' Tournament. The Augusta National Invitation was the name printed on the tickets, but in reality the 1934 tournament, like all those that followed, was the Masters. Jones finally relented five years later and the official name became the Masters in 1939.

Getting the tournament off the ground required not only big decisions, but attention to details such as course preparation, tournament infrastructure, publicity, hiring tournament workers, and much more (with the club in dire financial straits, this included determining which bills to pay). Roberts again took a leave of absence from his work in New York, moving to Augusta in November 1933 and staying there through the tournament except for a two-week period in February. "It is to Mr. Roberts that people go to for everything from the smallest detail to the major problems," the *Chronicle* noted.

Jones, of course, as president of the club, was in frequent communication with Roberts and involved in decisions. It wasn't quite a two-man show. Jay R. Monroe was an Augusta National member from New Jersey who at his other club, Baltusrol, had been very involved in running the 1926 U.S. Amateur. He paid an extended visit to Augusta in December to help with tournament matters. Rice also was involved.

Augusta National officially opened for its second season on November 20, 1933, but four days before that a special group played the course. The Spalding equipment company, with which Jones was associated, arranged for six top tour pros to travel to Augusta after a tournament in Pinehurst, North Carolina, and get a look at the course. Tommy Armour, Horton Smith, Joe Kirkwood, Craig Wood, Al Watrous, and Frank Walsh each spent two or three days in Augusta and were suitably impressed with Alister MacKenzie's layout.

Kirkwood said he had found something new there—even after playing more than 2,400 courses in a career that had taken him on exhibition tours around the world. Walsh said the course was just as good as MacKenzie's creation at Cypress Point in California, while Watrous called it America's finest inland course. Smith set a course record with a 67 and was impressed with the way the greens were protected largely with mounds instead of traps.

Two other interesting groups followed in the ensuing weeks. The Warner Brothers, Harry and Albert, along with two other executives of their company, visited in early December to spend a week playing golf, at the urging of Jones. They were impressed enough with the beauty of the course to say it would be used for a third series of film shorts to be produced in the spring (those never happened). They also had great praise for Augusta as a winter destination, which the *Chronicle* duly and enthusiastically reported.

The Warners suggested that the Augusta winter season, which started sometime between January 1 to January 10 with the opening of the Bon Air-Vanderbilt and Forrest Hills hotels, should open around Thanksgiving. The short season was an indication that Augusta was having some difficulties because the Depression reduced the number of travelers, and maybe even starting to lose its grip as a winter destination.

The *Chronicle* tempered its usually rosy outlook in an article about the hotels opening for the season, stating that "a fairly good tourist season is anticipated." And this was with the considerable boost anticipated by the first Masters.

In seemingly every article and editorial about the Masters, the newspaper pointed to Rice's estimate of 20,000 visitors spending a total of $1 million at Augusta businesses during tournament week, which became gospel. "If as many come as we are expecting, they will crowd the city from one end to the other," said Mayor Thomas Barrett, "and will be taken care of only by the fullest exertion of our powers of Southern hospitality." A housing bureau was set up to make sure that the expected throng of visitors could all find accommodations, with Augustans asked to make spare bedrooms available.

Another recurrent theme was that the Masters and Augusta National would turn Augusta into the winter golf capital of the country. Even Roberts got into the Augusta-boosting act.

"Many people are afraid of possible earthquakes and will not return to California, while Cuba, because of its internal strife, is out of the question this winter, and very few Americans are going to sell their dollars at forty percent discount in order to spend their winter vacations in Europe," said Roberts in November 1933, conveniently ignoring Augusta's biggest competitor for the tourist trade, Florida.

The next noteworthy group to arrive in town consisted of prominent Augusta National members Rice, Jones, Robert P. Jones, and Monroe, who came to discuss tournament plans. (The *Chronicle* was happy to point out that since joining Augusta National, Monroe was now wintering in Augusta instead of Florida, where he had spent his twenty previous winters.)

The foursome must have discussed tournament invitations. Originally, the field was supposed to be selected by a group of sports writers, but nothing was happening on that front. In the end, the club decided to form its own invitation committee.

Even then, they didn't seem to be in a hurry. The only immediate announcement was a list of twelve foreign invitees. This had some significance because American tournaments rarely thought about attracting international players, and it signaled what would become a long-term commitment in that regard. On the other hand, it was somewhat of a hollow gesture. Considering the world-wide economic situation, it hardly seemed likely that players would travel from all corners of the globe for a one-tournament trip to America, even if that tournament was hosted by Bobby Jones.

The invited players were Henry Cotton, Percy Alliss, Syd Easterbrook, George Duncan, Abe Mitchell, and Michael Scott of Great Britain; Aubrey Boomer and August Boyer of France; T. Miyamoto and R. Asamo of Japan; Jose Jurado of Argentina; and Ross Somerville of Canada. None of the overseas players accepted the invitation, though the amateur Somerville did make the shorter trip from north of the border to play in the tournament. (Two lesser players from England ended up being invited later and joining the field.)

As of February 14, less than five weeks before practice rounds would begin for the first Masters, invitations *still* hadn't been issued, according to the *Chronicle*. On March 3, just fifteen days before the first scheduled practice round, Roberts finally released a partial list of invitees that included just twenty-two leading pros and amateurs (the invitations had been sent out sometime in February). Of those, only fifteen ended up playing in the tournament.

*PGA Magazine*, a publication directed at the pros, said in an item on the upcoming Augusta event, "Players who receive invitations should reply promptly and if at all possible to do so, accept, and help Jones make this an outstanding event."

But even the weekend before the tournament, there were still question marks as to who would be playing. Some players who were expected to arrive never showed up, while others didn't make their decision until days before the Masters began. The biggest absentee was Gene Sarazen, winner of the 1932 U.S. and British Opens and 1933 PGA Championship (plus three earlier victories in those major events). He had responded to his invitation, writing that he would be glad to accept. Maybe at that point he hadn't checked the itinerary of his scheduled tour of South America with Joe Kirkwood. It turned out that Sarazen and Kirkwood had to miss the Masters because they were departing on the Tuesday of Masters week.

The peripatetic Kirkwood, a fine player better known as a trick-shot artist, was always looking for partners on his exhibition tours, which is where he made most of his money. When Sarazen became a hot commodity thanks to his major triumphs in the early 1930s, Kirkwood brought him along on a 20,000-mile swing around the United States in 1933. Then Kirkwood arranged the mother of all golf jaunts, a ten month, 120,000-mile around-the-world odyssey that started in South America and continued on to Europe, Canada, the Far East, and Australia, with competitive stops at various national opens along the way (including a quick stop back in the States for the U.S. Open).

Another big name missing was Tommy Armour, winner of the 1927 U.S. Open, 1930 PGA Championship, and 1931 British Open. Still a viable competitor at age thirty-eight (though his graying hair changed him from the "Black Scot" to the "Silver Scot"), Armour, who would win twice later in 1934, sent word that he was too busy at his club in Boca Raton, Florida, to be able to make it.

Olin Dutra missed the Southeast portion of the tour due to his duties at Brentwood Country Club in Los Angeles, so he couldn't play—he would win the U.S. Open two-and-a-half months later. Willie Klein of Miami's La Gorce Country Club was another tied down by responsibilities.

Still, seventeen of the top twenty players from the previous season were in the field, with only Sarazen, Kirkwood, and twenty-two-year-old Ralph Guldahl, the runner-up in the 1933 U.S. Open, absent. PGA manager Robert Harlow said that if it weren't an invitational, five hundred pros would have wanted to play.

Naturally, Jones wanted amateurs to be a big part of his tournament, but a number of them declined invitations. Unlike the pros, they weren't already in the vicinity anyway. Either the expense of the long trip or the fact that amateurs in the northern part of the country hadn't even begun their season led to the absenteeism. Francis Ouimet of Massachusetts, the 1913 U.S. Open and 1914 and 1931 U.S. Amateur champion, was certainly a player Jones wanted to see in the field, but he didn't make it. Neither did Johnny Goodman, the Nebraskan who had upended Jones at the 1929 U.S. Amateur and scored another upset by beating the pros to capture the 1933 U.S. Open.

After very publicly billing the tournament as featuring an elite field, the club quietly invited more players than it had indicated it would, including some with questionable credentials. Augusta Country Club pro David Ogilvie Jr. was in the field, as was local amateur W. D. "Dub" Fondren. PGA president George Jacobus and past president Charlie Hall were invited as players, and so were unheralded amateurs such as Bayard Mitchell and Sam Perry. More understandable was the presence of past U.S. Open and U.S. Amateur champions on the invitation list, but that included some players who were no longer competitive. In the end, there were twenty-four players—a full third of the field—who did not record a single round better than 76 in the tournament, and twenty-two who played in 1934 and never were invited again.

Then there was the strange case of Major General A. C. Critchley of England, a World War I hero who had gone on to become a sports impresario in Britain. He was mentioned as a competitor in a couple of pre-tournament reports and listed in the pairings, but his scores never appeared in the results.

Most of the players found accommodations at one of the resort hotels, which offered them special rates: the Bon Air-Vanderbilt was $5.50 a night, the Forest Hills $4.50, and the Partridge Inn $4. Not bad—but remember that only twelve players would finish in the money. Many pros halved their hotel expenses by rooming together.

Jones always stayed at the Bon Air-Vanderbilt on his Augusta visits. As tournament host, this allowed him to socialize with his fellow players during Masters week. But out at Augusta National, nobody expected Jones to be just a ceremonial golfer. The press angle going into the tournament was the same as ever in an open event—could the pros beat Jones?

Associated Press sports editor Alan Gould wrote that the pros entertained "more hope than convictions" that they could beat Jones. While there were some who thought Jones might just be going through the motions after sitting out since the summer of 1930, Gould wrote, "I would feel confident in his old competitive spirit asserting itself. No performer dominant for so long as Jones was could sensibly feel other than a strong urge to do his absolute best in attempting even a transient comeback.

"Championship golf . . . is not like boxing in respect to the angle that a long layoff is so costly in speed, stamina, and competitive edge," Gould wrote. "I'll be surprised if he doesn't finish among the first three at Augusta."

For some, it was as if Jones hadn't been away. Bobby Jones was Bobby Jones, and he would be hard to beat. Most people felt *almost* that way, but with a nagging doubt in the back of their minds about the effects of such a long layoff. But Horton Smith was bold enough to say that he and his fellow pros wouldn't fear Jones the way they used to, and his presence would have no effect on their game.

"Mechanically, Jones is playing as well as ever," Smith told the AP's Dillon Graham. "But the mental strain will be heavy. It may be hard for him to get back his perfect concentration."

When it came to beating Jones, the pros had strength in numbers. "The pace is faster than the days Jones played," said Smith. "I believe the leading professionals are twenty-six percent improved. There are more good pros now and the boys at the top just naturally have to shoot lower scores to get in the money."

Not that Smith was dismissive of Jones's chances. Even while saying that Jones was "not invincible," he said Bobby should be listed as a co-favorite with Paul Runyan at 8 to 1. Denny Shute should be 9 to 1 and about a dozen pros, "perhaps even including me," at 10 to 1.

Jones would be coming into the tournament cold in terms of competitive play, but he was taking his preparation seriously. He visited Augusta for three days in early February and then again in early March. During the latter visit he gave justification to those calling him the favorite, as he set the course record on March 3 with a 65—a round that included five birdies, an eagle, and no bogeys.

The Emperor had rarely gone that low even in his prime, but steel shafts were now helping him produce the lower scores he would need to be a contender at the Masters. Fearing an adjustment period, Jones had stuck with hickory in his Grand Slam year of 1930 even as others were switching to steel, which the USGA had legalized in 1926. He made the change after retirement when he was heavily involved with the design and production of his line of Spalding steel-shafted irons and woods. Jones found that some adjustment to his swing were necessary with the woods (the adjustment had long since been made by the time of the Masters) while it was a perfectly smooth transition with his irons.

Jones returned to Augusta on March 14 to play practice rounds on each of the eight days leading up to the tournament, except for a rain-out on Monday, while also consulting with Roberts on final preparations and greeting players as they arrived.

Only one player used hickory shafts in the Masters—forty-four-year-old Macdonald Smith, who represented an ultimately unsuccessful company in Nashville that made only hickory-shafted clubs. No player had been more bedeviled by Jones, having finished second to him in both the British and U.S. Opens in 1930—titles Smith had never won. "Mac" created an early sensation in Augusta by shooting a 66 in a practice round the Saturday before the tournament.

But the player people were talking about coming into the tournament—other than Jones—was Runyan. The twenty-five-year-old was fresh off his best performance yet, a sizzling 273 total posted in Charleston the week before the Masters, one of the lowest 72-hole scores ever shot. It was already his third win of 1934 after nine wins the previous year.

Runyan's 65 in the final round at Charleston still had people talking as the tour arrived in Augusta, fellow pro Charles Lacey calling Runyan the best putter that ever lived, an opinion seconded by O. B. Keeler after watching him play for the first time. But the relatively unassuming Runyan played down expectations.

"Although I really am playing pretty consistent golf now," he said, "I wouldn't regard myself as better than a 12 or 14 to 1 bet, no better than several other professionals."

Nearly everyone else disagreed, with Runyan universally touted as the co-favorite with Jones. Bookmakers—yes, they were a part of the scene in those days—installed both Runyan and Jones at 6 to 1. Next on the list were Macdonald Smith and 1933 British Open champion Shute at 8 to 1 followed by Horton Smith, Craig Wood, and Willie Macfarlane at 10 to 1. Word came on Tuesday that Runyan and Jones would be paired for the first two rounds as the leading gallery attraction. Calcutta betting, an auction type of pool where participants bid on players, was prominent in those days, with the biggest Calcutta at the Bon Air-Vanderbilt. Jones fetched the highest bid, $680, followed by Runyan at $550.

There were troubling signs coming from Jones as the tournament approached. On Monday he complained that he hadn't been making any long putts in his practice rounds—and then in the next two days his putting woes were extended to the shorter ones.

After shooting in the 60s a couple of times the previous week, Jones had his worst practice round on Tuesday, shooting a 76 as he and partner Augusta National pro Ed Dudley were drilled by Runyan and Horton Smith, 6 and 5, in a best-ball match. On Wednesday, he teamed for a 76 with amateur Somerville in the alternate-shot competition. Granted, Somerville was not in form after coming down from Canada (he would finish tied for 43rd in the tournament), but Jones didn't help much, and he even missed an 18-inch putt on the last hole.

After the round, Jones solicited help from Bobby Cruickshank and Macfarlane on the practice green. Cruickshank suggested that Jones should stand up straighter instead of leaning out over his toes.

"I've tried standing up, and sitting down," Jones lamented, "and I think the only way I'll ever be able to putt again will be from a sandbag rest. Like shooting a rifle."

Jones stayed at it for an hour, without much success.

"Ah, well—today's only today!" Macfarlane said.

Neither practice nor tips had really done the trick. Jones could only hope that his putting touch would somehow return overnight.

The eyes of the national golf press would be on him. The Masters drew the kind of coverage usually reserved only for the U.S. Open. The Associated Press sent its sports editor, Gould, along with Southeast writer, Graham; from New York came Paul Gallico, Kerr Petrie,

Joe Williams, and Lester Rice (but not William D. Richardson of the *New York Times*, which instead had reports from an unnamed correspondent); from Chicago were Joe Davis and Harvey Woodruff. Reportedly, sixty writers were expected, although, like so many figures, that might have been inflated. That number would have made for cramped quarters on the clubhouse veranda, where the writers worked by day. Their nighttime headquarters was the Bon Air-Vanderbilt, where they gathered to tell stories and sometimes mingle with the players.

The Columbia Broadcasting System was on hand for live radio coverage for fifteen minutes a day. The only tournament ever to have been broadcast live was the 1930 U.S. Open. CBS required that Augusta pay for the necessary equipment, leading to another mad scramble for funds just three weeks before the tournament. With Augusta National strapped for cash, Mayor Barrett formed a committee to raise money from private individuals, stressing the advertising value for the city of a nationwide radio broadcast. With sports announcer Graham McNamee unavailable, the broadcast was handled by former USGA president Herbert H. Ramsay.

The club produced an attractive souvenir program, with descriptions of the holes by MacKenzie from a 1932 story in the *American Golfer* and a piece about the history of the property by L. E. and P. J. A. (Louis and Allie) Berckmans. The local hotels bought ads, of course, but the rest of the advertising was an eclectic mix of New York hotels, national corporations, and companies that had been involved in the construction of the course. The latter were represented because the club still owed them money—they didn't have to pay for the ads, but the club did deduct the amount from what it owed.

There were ads for Buckner Hoseless Fairway Watering, the Evans Implement Company, the McWane Cast Iron Pipe Company, Pennsylvania Lawn Mowers, and the Florida Humus Company, mixed in with those for the Warner Brothers movie *Wonder Bar*, Quick Quaker Oats, Texaco, the St. Regis and Beverly Hotels in New York, and on the back cover the Monroe Calculating Machine Company (Jay Monroe's company). Roberts envisioned the program as a revenue-producing opportunity, intending it not only for tournament patrons but also for the several thousand visitors that he said dropped by the club during the year to take a look at the place. The program did turn a profit, but the club stopped putting one out after the first two years.

One more indication that the Masters was special was chartered flights from Atlanta to Augusta on the four tournament days, available for $15 round trip. Highway travel in those days, it should be pointed out, was not as easy because there was no Interstate 20 to hop on for the 150-mile trip.

The inaugural Masters might have been put together in ad hoc fashion, required a mad scramble to come up with enough money to hold it, and failed to attract 100 percent attendance by the game's best players. But make no mistake: From its outset the Masters was a very big deal. And the reason for that was simple: the comeback of Bobby Jones.

# 8

## 1934 ROUNDS 1 AND 2/ FALL OF THE EMPEROR

---

**A**S THE FIRST DAY of the Masters dawned, one question loomed largest over the proceedings: Did the Emperor of Golf still have clothes? While the answer wouldn't definitively come in a single day, this first round would go a long way toward showing what Bobby Jones still brought to the table as a player.

The time for speculation and talk was finished. Now there would be numbers on a tournament scorecard.

It wasn't a long wait. Jones and Paul Runyan went off the first tee at 10:35, just thirty-five minutes after the first twosome of Ralph Stonehouse and John Kinder officially got the inaugural Masters underway.

The results were highly discouraging to Jones's supporters: The Emperor was naked on the greens. While striking the ball nearly as well as ever, Jones was practically helpless with the putter. Poor putting saddled him with a four-over-par 76, six strokes out of the lead and in a tie for 36th place.

"When it came to a short pitch, a chip shot or a putt, he was a struggling golfer working with a prayer and a dream," Grantland Rice wrote in his syndicated account of the round.

The featured twosome was followed by a crowd described by most reporters as about a thousand spectators. This was an answer to the second biggest question heading into the Masters: How many people would show up?

*Augusta Chronicle* sports editor Tom Wall estimated the crowd as approximately 5,000. That number was way off. The Jones gallery was estimated at a thousand, and most observers agreed that he drew the bulk of the crowd. Wall's own story stated that 900 automobiles passed through the entrance and that officials estimated an average of four occupants per car. That would make 3,600, but that number is inflated, too. It's unlikely there was anything close to an average of four occupants, and players, officials, and club members accounted for some of those cars and didn't contribute to paid attendance. Gate receipts suggest a paid crowd of about a thousand.

Officials proudly pointed out that vehicles with license plates from thirty-eight states and Canada entered the parking lot. While that included the cars of players, who came from all parts of the country, it was indeed an impressive figure, and showed that the tournament— thanks entirely to Jones—had instant national appeal, if not a very strong local base for attendance. And the size of the gallery, while small by today's standards and falling short of optimistic projections, was pretty good compared to other tournaments of the era.

We tend to imagine golf tournaments of those days as rather gray affairs, but that's because the only evidence we see is black-and-white photographs of jacket-and-tie-wearing crowds. Wall paints a more colorful picture of what the scene looked like.

"Men and women, young and old, were attired in apparel resplendent of a rainbow," he wrote in Friday's paper. "Luxurious garments of a brightly-colored hue were in profusion as society went on parade."

The crowd, he wrote, "reflected what the well dressed person will wear in 1934," an indication that this was more of a high society than a working-class crowd, with well-heeled winter visitors holding sway.

The weather was cool, with a crisp breeze that tested the players and allowed players and spectators alike to show off their outerwear—Jones wore a checked blue sweater and Runyan a tomato-red sweater; both had matching long socks to go with their plus-fours. The fans weren't just there to see and be seen. While a few might have lingered in the area of the clubhouse, most set out to follow Jones in his return to competition. With no grandstands to camp in, that meant hoofing it around the course.

For gallery control the tournament recruited students from Richmond Academy high school, who wore cadet uniforms. Spectators walked down the fairways in those days, and they were kept from crowding too close to swinging players by the students holding long bamboo poles.

Jones—the "eminent Georgia barrister," as labeled by Alan Gould of the Associated Press—treated his fans to some magnificent shots with his woods. Having lost none of his prodigious power off the tee, Jones took advantage of his own course design by going for the green in two on all four par fives.

He had a chance for what could have been a seminal early moment on the fourth hole, known today as the famed 13th. Playing into the wind, he crushed a drive of 280 yards around the corner of the dogleg and then hit his fairway wood to within 15 feet of the hole. Alas, he missed the eagle putt. On the downhill, downwind, par-five 11th hole he boomed a drive of 300 yards and hit a brilliant second shot to within four feet, but again missed the eagle try. (Holes in this account are referred to by their 1934 numbers; with the nines the reverse of what they are today.)

Jones also reached the green in two on the par-five 17th, but three-putted from 45 feet to make a par. He boldly went for the green on the sixth despite a less-than-long drive, and came up short with his second, narrowly missing the water hazard which was then a stream instead of the pond that is there today. He ended up with a par.

O. B. Keeler, who had witnessed and described nearly Jones's entire career, wrote that the round featured "the finest driving I have ever seen Bobby produce." (It should be noted that Keeler's accounts were so liberally sprinkled with such "best ever" references that they should be taken with a grain or two of salt.)

The putting was some of the worst: Jones completely lost his touch on the short ones and missed an astounding seven putts of five feet or less.

Jones pulled no punches in describing his own putting woes in a conversation with Rice after the round. "I had no putting stroke at all," he admitted. "I honestly dreaded to look at a three or four foot putt, because I didn't feel that I could hole it. The rest of my short game wouldn't have been so bad if I could have side-stepped this nightmare on the greens.

"If my long game had not stayed with me I could not have broken eighty. If you can't putt in this game you can't get far. I hope to be better, for I know I can't be worse around the greens, not even if I use my shoe or an old rake."

There was some speculation that his putting implement was part of the problem. Jones had given his old reliable putter, Calamity Jane, to Spalding to use as a model for its replica putters. (It was inaccurately reported that Jones had sent the club to the Royal & Ancient Golf Club for display in St. Andrews, Scotland; actually, he had sent his old driver.) Now unexpectedly pressed back into competitive service at his own tournament, he was using the steel-shafted Spalding model.

Keeler even heard it suggested that Jones "quit using the new thin-shelled, high-powered ball he has used up to this season. I mentioned this to Bobby, of course. He asked what I thought about it. I said well maybe if he could get a ball with a different shape it would help. But I don't think he will change."

Jones's iron play wasn't as precise as it could have been. His distance control was off, as he overshot several greens and came up short of some others. He was fortunate on the third hole (today's 12th) that his tee shot didn't roll back into Rae's Creek, instead settling into long grass next to the front bunker.

Jones saved par on that hole to preserve a good start. Indeed, even with the shaky putting, his round didn't turn disastrous until near the end. His two-putt birdie on No. 4 got him to one-under, and while he gave it back with a bogey on the next hole from short of the green he finished with an even-par 36 on the front nine that included seven pars.

Jones's every stroke was being reported to the Associated Press via a short-wave radio setup, with a man named "Goat" Saxon following the match and calling in the results to writer Gould. When the twosome of Jones and Runyan reached the turn (Runyan a stroke ahead with a 35), the AP transmitted a story reporting on their front nine for that afternoon's newspapers.

Things took a turn for the worse on the 10th hole when Jones left himself behind some trees with his drive and ultimately made a bogey. Even his birdie on the next hole was disappointing, as that was his missed eagle opportunity, and he bogeyed the 12th when he missed a four-footer.

Jones bogeyed two of the next four holes when he ran afoul of mounds he and MacKenzie had built into the greens, three-putting the 14th and over-shooting the green on the 16th, where the pin was located just past the mound in a very difficult position. In between, he managed to shake in a six-foot birdie putt on the 15th to get back to one-over for the round.

The bogey at the 16th hole dropped him to two-over with two to play, and he stayed that way with the three-putt par on the 17th. Since in the end nobody broke 70 that day, Jones wasn't in terrible shape at that point. But he concluded his round with an ugly double bogey that had to be especially disheartening after a downhill drive of almost 300 yards into the fairway.

Jones made a mess of it from there, knocking a short iron over the green, stubbing a chip that failed to reach the putting surface, chipping four feet past, and (of course) missing from there. It added up to a 40 on the back nine.

In preparing for the tournament, Jones had shot par or better in nearly all of his rounds at Augusta National, and as low as 65. But he began to stumble as the tournament approached and when the bell rang, he proved the dictum that he had earlier written in his book, *Down the Fairway*: "There are two kinds of golf: golf—and tournament golf. And they are not at all the same thing."

Keeler tried to strike an optimistic note in his report, opening it by noting that Jones had been in a nearly identical position after the first round of the 1927 U.S. Open, six strokes behind and tied for 36th, and he ended up winning. But even Bobby's Boswell—as Keeler was known—had to admit this wasn't the *same* Jones.

"That Jones was a youngster in the first rush of the greatest career competitive golf has ever known; a Jones with the world of sport before him; a Jones with nerves of steel wire, tuned to concert pitch for the smashing cords of the 'Marche Militaire,'" he wrote. "The difference—well, the difference is being at concert pitch."

Rice, who through his Augusta connection was now just about as close to Jones as Keeler was, wrote that Jones "ran into a natural fit of nervousness on his first stage appearance after a long layoff. I have an idea that he will be something like the old Bobby Jones for the rest of the journey."

Jones was seen on the practice putting green for an hour late Thursday afternoon, trying to regain the touch. Writer Bill Wallace saw him leaving the course at 6:45 that evening, carrying his putter. "What are you going to do with that putter?" Wallace asked.

"I'm going to take it home to see if I can't get it heated up," Jones replied. "I'm going to sleep with it and if the putter and I have a good night's rest I'm going to play with it tomorrow."

The other half of the feature pairing also didn't put his best foot forward in the first round. Runyan was the first test case for how well a short hitter could hang in with the long knockers at Augusta National. Faced with the disadvantage of having to lay up on the par fives while Jones was going for the green, Runyan's putting was not enough to make the difference as it was not up to its usual standard on this day. Like Jones, he faltered on the back nine, following his opening 35 with a 39 coming home for a 74.

Still, in a bylined column for United Press, Runyan wrote, "It was one of the most enjoyable days I have had on any course" because of the chance to play with Jones in front of a large gallery. Runyan praised Jones's play with the woods, but wrote, "Before the tournament started I was of the opinion that Bobby's long stay in retirement would do something to his confidence under fire. I still feel that this is true, for he appeared very nervous, stopping on several occasions to wait impatiently for cameras to stop grinding and for the gallery to quiet down. . . . He needs a few rounds under his belt to get into the best competitive frame of mind."

MAKING THE MASTERS

Looking back on it many years later, Jones pinpointed two early moments that let him know he wasn't ready. Describing a 25-foot putt on the second hole, he wrote in *Golf Is My Game*, "I swung the putter back, but I gave it a jerk as I hit the ball and it went about two yards past the hole. I holed the next, but again I felt the jerk. I think I knew then what was coming."

Then on the fifth tee, "I was aware that the nervousness was still with me and may even have been increasing all the while. This was definitely not normal, because in the past it would have disappeared within a hole or two. I think the uncertainty I felt about my putting was the one thing that kept me from settling down. I realized that on that particular course if I could not become comfortable on the greens, I had no chance to work out a score . . .

"Anyway, as I stepped up to hit the tee shot on the fifth tee, a motion-picture camera started whirring, and I stepped away from the ball. Ordinarily, again, this would have been only a momentary distraction, but now I could not take hold of myself as I had done before. I hit the tee shot before I had completely settled down and pushed it into the woods on the right.

"At that very instant I realized that this return to competition was not going to be too much fun. I realized, too, that I simply had not the desire nor the willingness to take the punishment necessary to compete in that kind of company."

While Jones and the game's current hot young player faltered, the lead was shared by the player who was the hot youngster some five years previously. Horton Smith had burst on the scene spectacularly on the winter tour of 1928–29 as a twenty-year-old fresh out of Missouri. But he found that early brilliance difficult to maintain, and he had won only once each year in 1931, 1932, and 1933.

Still, when Smith shared the lead with a first-round 70 that included an eagle on the 17th hole it was pointed out that he was the last professional to beat Jones in a tournament. That happened at the 1930 Savannah Open before the Emperor reeled off victories in his last five tournaments, including all four legs of the Grand Slam. Also shooting 70s were forty-seven-year-old Emmet French, known mostly for finishing runner-up to Sarazen at the 1922 PGA Championship, and thirty-year-old Jimmy Hines, a Long Island pro who had just won his first tour event the previous year.

That nobody was able to break 70 was attributed to the capricious winds combined with the difficulty of the course. But there was another element at play. Then, as now, members don't like to see their course torn up by low scoring in tournaments. There were numerous complaints about holes being located in unfair positions, in most cases because they were set in close proximity to mounds, which made it very difficult—if not impossible—to stop an approach shot close to the hole. These complaints didn't come only from the players; writers chimed in, too.

"In my opinion, the flags were in bad spots at the first, third, and eighteenth greens," Keeler wrote, "and in worse spots at the twelfth and sixteenth, the twelfth being worst of all."

In his humorous daily account in the *Chronicle* under the pen name "Fairway Bill," Wallace referred to the 19th-hole clubhouse area where the players gathered after their rounds as the "sob room," and the main reason for the sobs on that day were the pin positions.

"The pros that shot them seventies, and seventy-ones, and seventy-twos, didn't have much to say," he wrote, "but, Boss, you should have heard them guys that were up there close to the 80 mark. They couldn't understand why they three putted so many greens. . . . Taking pity on [the] hole placing chairman, I suggested that he disappear from the 19th hole before some enraged golfer who had five putted a green would come in and use his niblick on the diaphragm."

The greens chairman was Monroe, who responded later in the week that the course was set up as a championship layout, which meant that the pins were in tough spots, but the course was the same for everybody.

Cagey veteran Walter Hagen found a way around the challenge at the 16th. With the pin placed diabolically behind a mound where "the good St. Andrew himself could not have stopped a ball from a position near the middle of the fairway," according to Keeler, Hagen deliberately aimed his tee shot 50 yards to the right, down the parallel eighth fairway. With the mound not in play from there, he hit his second shot inside 10 feet and made the birdie putt.

"You know you must play this game a little bit with the head, the rest with your clubs," said the Haig.

Within a couple of decades, the narrow fairway of that hole (No. 7 after the nines were switched to their present configuration in 1935) had become the most claustrophobic on the course, as tall trees grew up on each side of the fairway. But in 1934 it was wide open, some players opting for Hagen's route, which required hitting over some small trees; and others going to the left, down the 17th fairway. Most, however, played it straight.

At the age of forty-one, Hagen was no longer the force he was when he claimed two U.S. Opens, four British Opens, and five PGA Championships between 1914 and 1929. But he was still capable of winning the occasional tournament (his last victory would come in 1936) and with his flamboyant personality was still a gallery draw.

Hagen gave fans a treat with a 71 in the first round, five strokes ahead of Jones and only one out of the lead even though he was playing with a wrist he had injured a few days before. Rice called it "a marvelous performance."

The saga of Jones and his putting continued on Friday. After his long practice session the previous evening, Jones came out on Friday morning and spent another hour on the practice green before his afternoon tee time. He raised the hopes of onlookers by holing putts with impressive regularity, but gave an indication as to his mindset by saying, "I hope I don't leave this luck on the practice green."

That's exactly what happened. If anything, Jones was worse on the greens in the second round than the first. He three-putted three times, took a total of 38 putts, and even missed twice from a mere 18 inches.

Again things got worse as the round progressed, culminating in successive three-putts on the 14th and 15th holes followed by a missed birdie try from 18 inches on the 16th. The AP's Gould wrote that Jones's "hands seemed to shake" and Keeler wrote that he "stabbed jerkily at the ball," which sounds like the malady that today we know as the yips, where short putts become the thing of nightmares as hand control goes away.

Syndicated columnist Joe Williams insisted that Jones's miss on the 16th was from a mere foot. "Would you think it possible for the great Jones to miss a one-foot putt? I wouldn't either, if I hadn't seen it with my own eyes," he wrote. "Some of the boys said it was an 18-inch putt. But when was it ever necessary to debate inches on a Jones putt? As a compromise, I will grant it was a 15-inch putt. Still, he missed it."

Discussing it later with veteran pro Bobby Cruickshank, Williams suggested that the miss must have been due to carelessness. "On the contrary, he was never more careful in his life," said Cruickshank, who was familiar with Jones's putting troubles after trying to help him on Wednesday. "His putting has become a nightmare to him. The shorter the putts are, the greater his fear that he will not be able to sink them."

"It's got so it's funny now," Jones said to a friend late in the round. Jones displayed that humor on the 17th green, where Runyan's ball was sitting five feet to the left of the hole as Jones faced a 25-foot putt. "Paul, I think you better mark that ball, because I can't tell where this one of mine is going."

The mood hadn't been so light on the front nine, where the good work on the practice green was wiped away with his first missed 18-incher on the second hole. Then came a double bogey on the fifth, where he faced a tough pitch from short of the green over a mound—and stubbed it, moving the ball only a few feet.

Inexplicably, someone in the gallery called out, "Good shot, Bob."

"Thanks," Jones responded, without looking up. But then he turned to a friend and said, with a forced smile, "I could shoot a man for that, the way I feel now."

Keeler himself was apparently feeling pretty sick at what he saw: After the fifth hole he headed to the Red Cross tent and asked for a quarter pound of aspirin.

Jones's ball-striking remained solid, especially on the par fives. He two-putted for birdies on the fourth and sixth, and also birdied the par-three 13th, where he sank a 10-footer for his only one-putt of the round. That got him to even par for the day, but the bogeys on 14 and 15 dropped him back to two over and he finished with a 74 and a 150 total.

He had slightly improved his standing in the field to twenth-eighth, but fell eight strokes out of the lead with 36 holes to play, leaving the pre-tournament co-favorite as a long-shot for the title.

"His 'touch' in the short game has deserted him, and that's all about it. It had deserted him several days before the tournament—and, to my way of thinking, a good while before that, in spite of the pretty rounds he did in practice ten days ago," wrote Keeler. "It might return over night, but that is unlikely. Experience, determination and the cool courage that is always the birthright of a champion will keep Bobby in there playing golf through the last half of the tournament. But only a miracle—only a sudden return to concert pitch—can drive him up to a Garrison finish on Sunday. And they tell me the day of miracles is past."

Keeler noted that the problem wasn't just putting. Not mincing words, he wrote, "Bobby's chipping has been deplorable."

Henry McLemore of United Press assessed Jones's situation this way: "He appears to have no more chance at winding up winner than a beefsteak in a dog pound."

"I honestly have been afraid of even a foot putt," Jones told Rice after the round. "I almost missed three of those today. . . . The minute I walked onto the green I had the jitters. Even the sight of that cup made me sick. It looked to be smaller than the ball I was putting. It looked like a thimble. When I got close to the cup I felt as if I was looking at the fangs of a rattlesnake."

The AP's Gould resuscitated the "pros against Jones" angle, writing that the pros were galloping toward their biggest golfing "kill" since they routed Jones at the 1927 U.S. Open.

Such a perception of his play was the risk Jones took in taking his game out of mothballs for a return to the national stage. Gould did acknowledge that Jones's role as tournament host, and his long absence from competition, took something out of him: "So far he has played exactly like a perfect host, happy to see his old friends having a good time but quite unequal to the personal job of keeping pace with them after a lapse of four seasons."

It wasn't an entirely bad day for players with Augusta National connections. The club's professional, Ed Dudley, became the first player to break 70 in the Masters as he shot a 69 for a 143 total. That pulled him within one stroke of the lead, now held outright by Horton Smith at 142 after a 72.

Dudley might have held the 36-hole lead if not for a mysterious incident in the first round when he thought his tee shot was in the fairway on the fourth hole—only when he got out there, his ball was nowhere to be found. He had to return to the tee for a stroke-and-distance penalty. But on this day the fourth hole propelled him to the most spectacular stretch seen in the Masters so far, as his birdie there was the first of six in a nine-hole span.

Other bursts of excitement were provided by Ralph Stonehouse, with a 33 on the front nine, and Canadian amateur Ross Somerville, who made the tournament's first ace at the 145-yard seventh hole. Stonehouse was a curiosity in that instead of using a putter, he used a chipper—or what he called a "semi-chipper"—on the greens. This was a club designed for use from the fringe, with a head similar to a putter except that it had enough loft to get the ball briefly off the ground before it started rolling. It was an idea that perhaps wasn't entirely crazy in an era when greens were not conditioned as well as they are today. He won the Miami Open with it earlier in the winter season.

On the whole, players were losing the battle with the course designed by Jones and MacKenzie—Somerville's scores of 82–78 being just one example. Of the seventy players who completed two rounds, thirty-seven had totals of eight-over 152 or worse.

Chilly temperatures—the high on Friday was 57 degrees—and a moderate breeze did nothing to help scoring. The players were still trying to figure out the best strategy for playing the holes, and having trouble reading how the putts would break on the slopes MacKenzie and Jones built into the greens.

"The course here has given us a big surprise. It's tougher than it looks," wrote Runyan in his column. "I would say that the course is difficult because of the treacherous placing of the pins. They're changed every day, and the tournament committee, so far, has not been at a loss for wicked spots in which to sink the cups."

One of Thursday's three co-leaders, French, blew up to an 83 in the second round and was not heard from again—he withdrew after 36 holes. Hines did better, shooting a 74, but it was Horton Smith who moved to the forefront, taking the lead with his 142 total.

A Missouri native now playing out of Chicago, he showed that the way to score at Augusta was to conquer the par fives. Those holes accounted for four of his five birdies on Friday, allowing him to turn an otherwise troublesome round into an even-par 72. He got one big break along the way. Smith's drive on the par-four eighth hole came to rest in an unplayable position in a drainage ditch, but after some deliberation by rules officials he was given a free drop and was able to escape with a par.

Tied with Dudley at one stroke off the lead was Billy Burke, the Connecticut pro who had been the last player to arrive. He only got into town Tuesday night, arriving with Mrs. Burke and a bloodhound named Jerry. Seeing the course for the first time on Wednesday, he teamed with Johnny Golden to win the alternate-shot competition with a 67, quite a good score with only one ball in play. Burke had managed only a couple of victories since taking the 1931 U.S. Open, but rounds of 72 and 71 had him very much in the picture here.

Burke's playing partner Hagen went in the wrong direction on Friday. After his first-round 71, the Haig stumbled to a 76 in the second round, hampered by wild driving such as a tee shot that found the creek to the left of the fourth fairway. It could have been even worse but Hagen still had the knack for extraordinary recovery shots—on the par-five 17th hole he drew a gasp from the gallery by smacking a brassie (the equivalent of a two-wood) second shot from soft ground in the woods and nearly reaching the green. Still, it was clear that the Masters would not be a reprise of the 1920s as a Jones–Hagen duel for the title was not in the offing.

They played together in the final two rounds, though. "I think I can help Bobby," Hagen said to Rice, who he knew was heavily involved in making the pairings. "I'd like to play with him."

Forty-four-year-old Macdonald Smith did have a chance, a prominent name joining Hines and Stonehouse at 144. Smith was considered the sweetest swinger in the game, which was perhaps the reason he stuck with hickory shafts. "The stylist of stylists," his friend Tommy Armour called him. But fate had dealt Smith cruel blows in national Opens, twice a runner-up on each side of the Atlantic—and that didn't even include the time an out-of-control gallery was largely blamed for his losing the 54-hole lead at the British in 1925.

"Macdonald Smith is the master artist of golf and the art of golf has denied him the laurels of national championships," Armour wrote. "This fickle and utterly irrational art has crowned as its rulers men who, as the game's artists, are merely caddies compared to the master."

Smith's career was a long and strange journey that included a playoff loss at the age of twenty to his brother Alex in the 1910 U.S. Open, one of his first tournaments in America after coming over from Scotland, and a mysterious gap from 1917 to 1923 when he disappeared from competition. He spent part of that time working in a shipyard and reputedly had a drinking problem, but a 1922 marriage helped turn his life around. From 1924 up until the 1934 Masters he had twenty-two victories, including a win at the Los Angeles Open two months earlier that stamped him as one of the favorites at Augusta.

But the national Opens had eluded him and he never entered the PGA Championship, apparently because he didn't like match play. The Masters wasn't considered a "major" yet, but the concept of four professional majors had yet to be established at that point. It can't quite be said that Smith was chasing a first major, but a win at the Masters would have been big for him at the time. (In retrospect, it would have been huge for him, as it would have wiped away the "best player never to win a major" tag, though Smith did win three Western Opens when that was considered a big deal.)

Runyan made a move forward on Friday with a 71 for a 145 total, tied with upper echelon players Craig Wood, Leo Diegel, and Al

Espinosa. Still, the tournament lacked some of the sizzle it would have had going into the weekend if Jones had been in serious contention.

Newspaper accounts didn't agree on who was the low amateur through two rounds. The AP's Gould had it as Johnny Dawson, a "'business man' amateur" five strokes out of the lead at 147. But Dawson, though he would not accept prize money, wasn't considered an amateur by the USGA because he sold and marketed golf equipment for Spalding, and thus made his living from the game. He was ineligible for the U.S. Amateur, and elected not to compete in the U.S. Open, although at one point Jones called him probably the greatest amateur golfer in the world.

Dawson did compete occasionally on the tour without accepting prize money throughout the 1930s, and also in some amateur events that didn't go along with the USGA's interpretation. He regained his USGA amateur status after turning to real estate as his profession in 1942, which was the same year he beat the pros to win the Bing Crosby Pro-Am tour event. He was runner-up in the 1947 U.S. Amateur, but perhaps made his biggest impact on the game as a real estate developer. Dawson was the visionary who first brought golf to what had been barren desert in Palm Springs, California, developing Thunderbird Country Club in 1950, and pioneering what would become a golf explosion in that area.

While by today's standards it seems harsh that Dawson wasn't considered an amateur because he worked for an equipment company, it's more understandable that Jones didn't have amateur status for the 1934 Masters. The game's iconic amateur competitor had undeniably cashed in on the fame he earned as a player by signing the lucrative Hollywood contract (and been paid to provide golf instruction, to boot). Not that he considered himself a professional player—when he agreed to enter the Augusta National tournament, he said that he would not accept prize money. Neither a real pro nor a real amateur,

Jones was sort of in limbo while assuming the unique role of tournament host. While nobody referred to him a professional, he did not get the asterisk in the tournament results in the *Chronicle* that indicated an amateur, nor did any of the writers consider him a part of the amateur field.

Keeler's report had the low amateur as Charlie Yates with a 148 total. That performance undoubtedly pleased Jones to no end, because twenty-one-year-old Yates was a protégé of his from East Lake and Georgia Tech. The Yates and Jones families both lived in houses bordering East Lake, and young Charlie started tagging along with Jones when Bobby became an amateur phenom.

"When I was about seven years old, I'd slip across the fence and watch him play," Yates recalled to the *Augusta Chronicle* in 2001. "He never seemed to mind. When he finished a match, sometimes he'd stand behind the 18th green and knock balls in the opposite direction. We boys would pick the balls up. That was a great treat.

"I remember one time we were following him and he was going into the clubhouse at the turn. He took me to the grill room and bought me a Coke."

When Charlie got older and became a fine golfer himself, he began to play with Jones at East Lake instead of following him. Yates won the Georgia Amateur in 1931 and 1932, and now here he was playing in his mentor's tournament—and beating him by two strokes.

That's not how Clifford Roberts, Thomas Barrett, and others behind the tournament who were looking to maximize gate receipts and publicity for Augusta would have scripted it. But while Jones was coming up short as a player, there were few complaints about the tournament he was hosting or the course that provided the stage. The Masters, if not Jones himself, was off to a good start.

# 9

# THE LEADER/THE JOPLIN GHOST

**IT WAS DISAPPOINTING THAT** Bobby Jones wasn't in real contention after 36 holes, but the tournament was led by a man who at one time was supposed to be the next Bobby Jones.

Horton Smith burst out of Missouri at the age of twenty in 1928–29 with such force that he still stands as the most accomplished player at an early age the PGA Tour has ever seen—including Tiger Woods. Here are the all-time Tour leaders in victories before a given age:

21st birthday—Horton Smith 8, Gene Sarazen 3, Tiger Woods 2
22nd birthday—Horton Smith 12, Tiger Woods 6, Gene Sarazen 4
23rd birthday—Horton Smith 14, Tiger Woods 7, Gene Sarazen 4
24th birthday—Horton Smith 15, Tiger Woods 15, Jack Nicklaus 8
25th birthday—Tiger Woods 23, Horton Smith 17, Jack Nicklaus 12

Smith was twenty-five at the time of the 1934 Masters. While he was playing too well to be called washed up, he *was* yesterday's news.

While his good friend Paul Runyan had stepped into the spotlight, Smith had slipped into the shadows. Now in a tournament featuring the return to competition of Bobby Jones, Smith was staging a comeback of his own—from relative mediocrity.

Smith had won only one tournament in the previous seventeen months, and that was with Runyan as his partner at the 1933, Miami International Four-Ball. The perception was that Runyan had done most of the heavy lifting there and carried Smith to victory. In a poll of forty-two PGA players taken in November 1933, not a single one voted for Smith as one of the top ten players.

When he was taking the tour by storm five years earlier, Smith was called the "Joplin Ghost" because he was based out of Joplin, Missouri, and he was exceedingly hard to catch once he had the lead. For much of the period 1931 to 1933 he was a ghost in the sense that his presence was barely felt.

Smith actually hailed from Springfield, Missouri, not Joplin. He spent his early years on a small farm seven miles outside of town before his family made the fortuitous move to a 31-acre farm directly across from Springfield Country Club.

His father, Perry, made his living primarily by buying and selling cattle, so what farming was done on their place was done by Horton, his older brother Ren, and his mother. As a result, Horton was hardened by farm labor but also had the advantages of being from a relatively prosperous family due to the success of his father's business.

One of those advantages was joining the country club. His father didn't play much golf, but got a family membership after Horton and Ren got into the game as caddies. Not that Springfield was an elite club with impeccably manicured fairways. In fact, Smith said that it wasn't until he started playing on the tour that he realized the fairways of a golf course ought to have playable lies. "This makes a great deal of difference," he told a reporter.

Springfield had sand greens, but Smith nonetheless became one of the best putters of his time. He said that learning the game on sand greens actually helped him, because being able to see the track of the ball not only enabled him to get a feel for the line of the putt but also to develop a level stroke—if he hit up on the ball too much, he could see how the ball skipped at the start instead of rolling; if he hit down on it, he could see where the blade of his putter contacted the sand.

The club's professional, Neal Cross, took Smith under his wing. When Horton was fifteen, Cross arranged for Horton to caddie for Walter Hagen in an exhibition match, and that same year Smith won the club and city championships. At sixteen, he was a semifinalist in the Western Junior. A bright kid and a good student, Smith matriculated at State Teachers College in Springfield. But he really wanted to apply his mind to what really fascinated him—the game of golf. What's more, he wanted to make it his profession, and felt that he had the ability to be successful at it.

"He saw in it the possibilities of a business career, just as others see the same promise in law, medicine, and finance," Joe Williams would write in the *New York Telegram* less than four years later when Smith had already made it big.

Given the small monetary rewards in golf compared to those other professions, it was a vision that was hard for others to see, including Horton's father, who said, "But there's no future, no money, nothing in golf."

"It will have a future if I am any good at it," Horton replied.

"Well, son, do whatever you like, but convince me as soon as you can that there is a future in it," said his dad.

Just before his eighteenth birthday in May 1926, Smith became an assistant pro and caddie master at Springfield Country Club and later that year showed his notion of making a living as a player was not a pipedream when he finished tenth in the Heart of America Open, a tour event in St. Louis. The next year he worked simultaneously at clubs in three Missouri towns on different days of the week and also qualified for the 1927 U.S. Open, making the cut at Oakmont less than a month after turning nineteen.

His ambition fired, Smith was able to get a Springfield man named A. H. Hill to advance him $1,000 so he could play the western and southwestern portions of the winter tour of 1927–28, telling him he felt he could make decent money on the circuit if he had some decent clothes, a good set of clubs, and enough cash so he wouldn't have to worry about getting home. "My dad could have let me have that money, but I would have felt like I was under pressure all the time if I was using his money to play," Smith said later. "But Mr. Hill had it and wanted to loan it."

Smith played in fourteen tournaments, finishing in the money in all but one. He broke even financially, while gaining valuable experience.

He parlayed that success to a better club job at Oak Hill Country Club in Joplin in 1928, with his older brother as his assistant. But the Joplin Ghost would only stay in Joplin for one season—by the next year his life had become a whirlwind of tournaments, exhibition matches, and public acclaim.

It all started in September in Kansas City, where the young pro made the field for the PGA Championship despite carding an eight and a nine on the second and fourth holes of the 36-hole qualifying. Still deep in the trees after six strokes on the fourth hole, Smith stooped down to pick up his ball and withdraw.

"All of a sudden I realized I was quitting," he later recalled. "I straightened up, grabbed a club, hit the ball out, made a nine with one putt, and kept going. That day made me. It taught me perseverance and to never give up and was a helpful thing the rest of my life. I've never forgotten that day. It changed my whole career."

Smith qualified with scores of 79–70—149 despite a 44 on his first nine holes. Then in the PGA Championship at Baltimore Country Club he made it to the semifinals. He was on his way.

Smith's first victory came a month later in November 1928 at the Oklahoma City Open. After losing a two-stroke lead on the first hole of the final round, Smith's lesson in perseverance paid off. He not only kept his cool, he hit a perfect shot on the par-three second hole and made a hole-in-one to take the lead for good.

"First prize was a thousand dollars," Smith recalled. "It seemed like a million to me."

Smith claimed his second win on Christmas Eve at the Santa Catalina Island Open in California. The tournament was held on a little nine-hole, par-32 course, but it was significant nonetheless because Smith outdueled Hagen, the game's glamour boy and best professional. Smith's scores of 63-58-61-63 gave him an 11-under 245 total, one ahead of Hagen and 11 strokes clear of third place as the two were the class of the field.

Hagen was so impressed with that showing and another Smith win at the Pensacola Open in early 1929 that he named the twenty-year-old to the United States Ryder Cup team that would compete in England in April. Since steel shafts were still outlawed in Great Britain (they wouldn't be legalized there until 1930), Smith decided to acclimatize himself to hickory shafts at the Belleair Open, which resulted in him finishing out of the money.

Going back to steel, Smith turned into a juggernaut, winning his next four individual tournaments. He beat Denny Shute in a playoff at the Fort Myers Open, where the two of them played 47 holes the final day—the last two regulation rounds, a scheduled nine-hole playoff that ended in a tie, and a hastily arranged agreement to play sudden death (a rare format for that era), which Smith won on the second hole.

After losing with partner Al Watrous in the match-play International Four-Ball, Smith captured the Florida Open in Jacksonville before heading to the richest event on the tour that year, Miami's La Gorce Open. Smith claimed the enormous first prize of $5,000 plus a $1,000 gold plate with a two-stroke victory over Ed Dudley.

Back home his father, who usually haunted the Associated Press room of the *Springfield News and Leader* on the final day of tournaments, stayed away this time. "I was afraid," he later told the paper. Horton was able to send the big winner's check to his father as proof that there was a future in golf—and that it hadn't taken long for him to show it.

Smith beat a field at La Gorce that included Hagen, Sarazen, reigning U.S. Open champion Johnny Farrell, Tommy Armour, Bill Mehlhorn, and virtually everybody who was anybody in golf, except, of course, for amateur Bobby Jones, the greatest player of them all.

Smith's spectacular run was earning him comparisons with Jones, and who better to make that evaluation than O. B. Keeler, Jones's chronicler and traveling companion? Keeler covered the tour's next event, the North and South Open in Pinehurst, North Carolina, and this is what he observed.

"[Smith is] cool, composed, as modest as a kid popularly is supposed to be and usually isn't, the best-looking youngster I have laid my eyes on since Bobby Jones was a boy wonder, and I can't say if he looks better than Bobby did at that age because they are radically different in all parts of style.

"Where Bobby is short and stocky, Horton Smith is tall and lanky. Where the Jones shoulders are broad and his chest is thick, the Smith shoulders are sloping. Curiously enough, the Smith swing is shorter than the Jones swing; Horton is just between a full and a three-quarters swing in the big shots, leisurely going back and coming through with a magnificent lashing impact. But where they do agree is a vital point—a perfectly straight left arm through all the shots until well after impact."

Smith shot a 67 in the morning round of the 36-hole final day at the North and South to propel him to a two-stroke victory over 1927 U.S. Open champion Armour. It gave him seven wins, along with three runner-up finishes, in eighteen tournaments on the five-month winter tour.

"He is a greater golfer than I expected to see and I expected to see a very great one," Keeler concluded.

With word circulating at Pinehurst that Jones was considering retiring, "The question of the Atlanta's successor naturally arose," wrote United Press sports editor Frank Getty. "At the moment it looks as if Horton Smith, at twenty, stood the best chance of filling Bobby's shoes as the outstanding golfer in the world."

Hagen wasn't so sure. Asked by a gallery member at the International Four-Ball how Smith compared with Jones, the Haig responded, "There's only one Jones. We'll never see another like him—at least we'll not live to see him."

Nonetheless, Hagen was very impressed by Smith, saying, "He's got every shot in the bag."

There was another thing that noted raconteur Hagen observed about the kid from Missouri. "He doesn't smoke, drink, or give a rap about girls," Hagen said. "I have yet to hear about the boy or girl who can keep him out after nine o'clock."

Asked whether Smith was missing out on a lot of fun by not mingling with "the boys," Hagen joked, "A helluva lot; he doesn't know he's alive," before adding, "But that is his business and I'm proud of him for it."

Indeed, Smith came across as a straight-laced country boy from America's heartland: modest and amiable, not displaying much of a personality or sense of humor but taking everything in with a pleasant grin and not letting much bother him.

"Despite his youth, he possesses the poise of a veteran," wrote John D. Nash in the *New York Post*. "All this adulation and gallery worship is new to him, but he accepts it gracefully, and always with that broad, infectious smile that has endeared him to thousands on his junket across the country. It must seem quite strange to this big country boy to have throngs clamoring at his heels, seeking his autograph, a scrap of paper he might let fall, a little tee—anything . . . that the lad possessed, to carry home as a souvenir.

"With each new conquest his popularity increases. Large galleries often serve to unsettle the most hardened vet, but Smith seems to blend perfectly with the crowd. If he is jostled, there is a smile for the culprit. Everyone calls him Horton, and with that rustic characteristic for familiarity, he seems to relish it."

Warren Brown of the *Chicago Herald and Examiner* wrote that Smith "is an easygoing youngster who refuses to let his golf bother him greatly, if at all. In temperament he is in some respects not unlike Walter Hagen. I have yet to hear Hagen explain what would have happened to his score if such and such had or hadn't taken place. Smith is like that. If he hits a bad shot, he doesn't let it dismay him. There is always another shot coming along.

"Smith has no conceit whatever. He is an extremely likeable youngster, always wearing a grin, as if he wonders what the fuss is all about."

Back home in Springfield, family friend Dr. Wilbur Smith said of Horton, "In all the years I've known him, I've never seen him hit the turf or use a profane word." The secrets to his success, Dr. Smith said, were "clean living, clean thinking, hard work, and an even disposition."

Another key to Horton's success was that he was a keen student of the game. He credited his improvement from his first winter tour to his domination in his second year to being able to observe the swings of other pros and talking to them about their technique. Later in 1929 when he made his first trip to Europe, he made sure to talk to past-his-prime British great Harry Vardon about the golf swing.

While learning from others, Smith developed an idiosyncratic technique that best suited his six-foot-one frame and the new steel shafts.

"There was very little question of the full, free-flowing type of swing [of which Jones was the prime example] being the ideal," Smith later wrote. "It didn't work for me though, and probably not for others of my type of build. I retained the essentials of my predecessors but worked out a relatively short swing which began giving me excellent results during the tournaments in 1929."

Indeed, Smith's backswing was the shortest of any of the top pros of the day. He wasn't one of the longer hitters (nor was he among the shortest), but he was very accurate. Hagen, who tended to be wild off the tee, admired Smith's "devilish straightness."

Hagen also said that Smith was Jones's equal on chip shots around the green. But it was on the putting surfaces that Horton stood out.

"Horton was the best putter I've ever seen," said Runyan, who himself had a deserved reputation as a great putter. "To mention anyone else in the same breath is a travesty. He planted himself parallel to the intended line and was sound technically. But what made him a great putter was his attitude. He had a dogged determination to do it the same way, week after week and year after year. Unlike everyone else, he never changed putters unless he was playing well. As he explained it to me, when he did change, he wasn't hoping. He was doing it with considered judgment. Then if he went back to the old putter, he did so with more confidence."

Runyan was on the mark about Smith's devotion to a single method. Associated Press writer Paul Mickelson made the mistake in 1934 of asking Smith if he had a new system of putting.

"No. When you get a sound system—a sound system I said—don't change it. Develop it," Smith replied. "That's the problem with a lot of excellent golfers. They get a sound putting touch, then they get a bad round and start experimenting. As a result, they get a hodgepodge system that ruins their game."

Smith was ahead of his time in giving a lot of thought to the psychology of the game. "What makes a man a champion in golf is the capacity for cooling and quieting the nerves at the right time," he wrote in a magazine article. "There are so many great players who are practically equal in the execution of all shots that we have to look to something besides technical ability to explain successful scoring performances.

"Each championship is two championships; one the championship that I play so people can see it and the other, the one that I have to play inside myself. If I can retain within myself a mental advantage over the rest of the field, I then can benefit from the confidence that shot for shot on the practice tee or green, I am as good as any of them."

Golf was seldom far from Horton's mind. When the members of the Ryder Cup team gathered for some sight seeing in New York before boarding a ship to England, Smith was having the sights pointed out to him from the roof of the New York Athletic Club when he was distracted by a niblick with a very large head that one of the party had with him. He immediately grabbed it and started hitting imaginary shots. "Have you ever seen a niblick like this?" he asked.

Smith was one of only two Americans to win his singles match at the Ryder Cup as the United States fell to Great Britain, but that was just the start of an extended stay in Europe. The British Open followed in early May, and Grantland Rice was sure that Smith could overcome the "hoodoo" that seemed to affect American stars from Walter Travis to John McDermott to Francis Ouimet to Walter Hagen and even Bobby Jones in their first British Open. "He has worked his way to an almost flawless swing. No man in golf hits the ball truer or better with every club," Rice wrote. "He also has a wise, cool head and a stout heart."

Alas, Smith succumbed to the weather—or the hoodoo—and finished twenty-first as Hagen took the claret jug. But moving across the English Channel to the French Open, Smith showed that the hype was justified. Nobody could remember a better one-day display of golf than his 66-66 in the first two rounds at St. Cloud Country Club in Paris, which gave him a twelve-stroke lead. "I've seen only two or three other persons to compare with him," said British pro George Duncan, who played with Smith. "Harry Vardon, Bobby Jones, and Walter Hagen."

The next day he strode to a comfortable victory and was greeted on the 18th green by Hagen holding a birthday cake, for Smith turned twenty-one that day. That evening he attended a party, where he was introduced to one of the guests, a young woman.

"Will you have a cigarette?" she offered.

"I don't smoke," he said.

"How about a drink?" she asked.

"Thanks, but I don't drink," he replied.

"Don't you have any bad habits?" she persisted.

"Yes, I'm short with too many putts."

Smith continued on to Germany, finishing second in the German Open before returning to the States. All eyes were on him at the U.S. Open, where he finally would compete in the same tournament as Jones. That proved to be a disappointment, as Smith finished in a tie for tenth, eight strokes behind Jones, who defeated Al Espinosa in a playoff.

There would be no need for Smith to return to his club job in Joplin. He had become enough of a celebrity that he was booked for a hundred exhibitions with Hagen. Eleven of those came on consecutive days leading up to the U.S. Open, leaving them with only two practice rounds—probably not the best preparation. The rest were packed into July through October, including one period of thirty-three consecutive days—and one event in Boston where they pitted their best ball against an archer shooting arrows from tee to green.

Though their personalities could hardly have been more different, and Hagen was fifteen years older, the two nonetheless hit if off and became good friends. Smith said of Hagen, "He enjoyed fancy clothes, a little drink, and the ladies, but it would have been absolutely impossible for him to have been a complete playboy and still maintain the physical and mental endurance required to play championship golf. Stories of his heavy drinking were exaggerated or false. He had a host of friends and enjoyed many parties with them. And he always had a drink in his hand. But one or two drinks would last a whole evening."

Stories of Hagen being late to the first tee weren't exaggerated, however. He was such a gate attraction—and a charmer—that he could get away with showing up late to tournaments (except for the U.S. and British Opens and the PGA Championship, where he was sure to be with on time). Smith said Hagen didn't do it for the purposes of intimidation or to gain attention.

"He was just the slowest individual I ever saw," said Smith, who at first was frustrated when Hagen was late for exhibitions but grew to accept it. "One day when Walter was shaving, I realized that we would be late. I urged him to hurry. He did nothing but smile and never hurried at all. Finally, he told me that if he expected to have a fine, smooth, unhurried stroke on the golf course that day, he did not think the proper method of getting himself into the tempo for the day would be by rushing his razor blade."

Hagen didn't play a full tournament schedule, but Smith went straight from his exhibition tour to nonstop travel on the winter tour. That earned him a new nickname: the Missouri Rover.

Smith won three times before the calendar turned, giving him a total of eight wins and $15,000 in earnings in 1929. Two more wins in the first three months of 1930 gave him five wins on the 1929–30 winter tour—not quite the haul of the previous winter but still impressive.

Along the way, he became the first pro to use a sand wedge and the last to beat Jones before the great amateur retired. Smith learned about the sand wedge in February 1930 from an acquaintance in Houston who introduced him to E. K. McClain, a cotton broker and average golfer who had invented a new kind of niblick designed to get the ball out of the bunker. It had a large, concave face and was very heavy, weighing twenty-three ounces.

McClain wanted to see if he could get one of the major manufacturers to make the club, and Smith, having recently signed with Hagen's new equipment company, said he would take a look at it. After getting good results with it, Smith convinced the company to manufacture the club.

The first tournament where Smith used the sand wedge was the Savannah Open, which was also a noteworthy event because of a memorable duel with Jones, who was using this event and another one in Augusta the following month as tune-ups for his bid at the Grand Slam. A mutual acquaintance arranged for Smith and Jones to room together in Savannah.

"It was the beginning of a long and close friendship, which has been a rich experience for me," Jones later wrote in *Golf Is My Game*. "Both on and off the golf course, Horton has always been a model of his profession and a credit to golf."

"Of course, we two roommates had a very good time together. I think we both liked one another from the beginning, and we had a lot of fun talking golf, practicing swings, and exchanging pointers in the room and going to movies in the evening after dinner."

The tournament became a game of "Can you top this?" between them. Jones set a course record of 67 in the first round, Smith established a new mark with a 66 in the second, and Jones came right back with a 65 in the third. The two were tied at 207 entering the final round. No course records were set in the final round, but Smith, knowing that Jones had completed play with a 279 total, parred his way home on the closing holes for a one-stroke victory. These two great players left the rest of the field far behind, with Jones six strokes ahead of third place.

Smith wasn't scheduled to play in the Southeastern Open in Augusta, but organizers were desperate to promote another duel between Smith and Jones. Smith was playing in the North and South Open in North Carolina on Tuesday and Wednesday (36 holes each day), and he was booked for exhibitions on Thursday and Friday in Charlotte and Asheville and then a golf-show appearance in Boston on Monday. The Southeastern Open was scheduled for Friday, Saturday, and Sunday.

Augusta Country Club president Fielding Wallace made an offer to Smith just three days before the scheduled start of the Southeastern Open. The Augusta tournament would be switched to a Saturday-Sunday affair, Smith would be given an early starting time on Sunday, and a plane would be provided at 2:00 P.M. for the four-hour flight to Washington, D.C., from where he could catch an overnight train to Boston. As an inducement, Smith would be guaranteed first-place prize money.

Smith accepted the offer, but undoubtedly wasn't at his best because of the harried travel schedule and the fact that he was playing on two courses that were totally unfamiliar to him (the first 36 holes were at Augusta Country Club and the final 36 at Forrest Hills). He and Jones were paired in the first two rounds and a large gallery watched Jones take the lead with a 144 total while Smith was at 148. Smith teed off at 6:45 AM the second day, so early that he completed his third round before Jones even arrived at the course. Smith finished with a 297 total that earned him low-pro honors—but he was 13 strokes behind Jones's winning score.

Smith didn't even learn of the final result until the next morning in Boston. His flight to Washington was not uneventful. Those were still early days for air travel and the pilot of the single-engine plane, though he had been described by Wallace as "one of the best pilots in America," had never been north of Charlotte. He got lost when they got near Washington, and since the plane didn't have much fuel left he decided to land in a field on a farm to ask for directions. Fortunately, they were good directions, and Smith arrived safely in Washington, and Boston, on time.

More opportunities were ahead for Smith, as he toured Britain for a series of exhibitions with American pro Leo Diegel before playing in the 1930 British Open. Smith did better at the Open this time, finishing fourth, while Jones won the second leg of the Grand Slam, incidentally using a sand wedge that Smith had McCain make for him after Jones expressed his interest in the club in Savannah.

Then it was another boat trip across the ocean and a train ride to Minneapolis for the U.S. Open. Smith led through two rounds at Interlachen with a 142 total, but he couldn't keep pace on the 36-hole final day, shooting 76-74 to finish third while Jones took the trophy. Failure to win the U.S. or British Open or the PGA Championship was the only blemish on Smith's record—but he had plenty of company in not being able to beat Jones in an Open.

Smith finally had a chance to visit home after being on the road for twenty straight months, a period in which he had traveled an estimated 41,000 miles while playing in some 130 exhibitions and fifty tournaments. Horton insisted at the time that he felt fresh, but soon his body began to break down. It was physical woes more than anything that led to his decline over the next few years.

He began to experience back problems in the fall of 1930 and couldn't shake them for several years, and even then not completely. Smith had to cut down considerably on his practicing and also alter his swing because of his back. He stayed competitive thanks to his outstanding short game, but never again struck the ball as consistently as he did from 1928 to 1930.

Along the way Smith also had a serious sinus infection that landed him in the hospital and a broken wrist in December 1931 that sidelined him for six months and continued to bother him for a while after that.

"Troubles, like triumphs, seem to run in flocks," he later wrote. "I began to think that the only championship I might even win would be that played by the patients of some hospital ward. . . . Maybe I had been grinding the machinery pretty hard without realizing it and was so worn down the back and sinus troubles might have been aggravated by the persistent playing strain."

The wrist injury occurred when Smith was a passenger in a car driven by Joe Kirkwood during a tournament in San Francisco. Smith stuck his arm out the window while Kirkwood was parking the car, and got his wrist caught between the car and a post.

It was the second part of a bookend of bad breaks for Smith in 1931. The first came when the USGA outlawed the concave sand wedge that January. The wedge had been a big seller when it hit the market in the summer of 1930, with Smith getting a 25-cent royalty on each club sold. That came to an end with the USGA ban.

Smith managed two victories at the end of 1930, giving him a total of fourteen in just twenty-six months. But he won only once in each of the next three years, and in 1933 it was a team victory with Runyan. No longer in demand for exhibitions, he took a club job at Oak Park Country Club near Chicago to occupy him during the summer months but continued to play a full schedule of tournaments when healthy.

Quietly, though, he was playing better on the winter tour of 1933–34. He hadn't won, but he was consistently finishing near the top, including a loss in the final of the International Four-Ball match play event, again with Runyan as his partner. Smith was ready to show that he was still a force to be reckoned with.

# 10

## 1934 ROUNDS 3 AND 4/
## SMITH AND JONES

---

THE THIRD ROUND WAS played on a raw, cloudy day with a high temperature of 52 degrees. Not exactly chamber of commerce weather for a town trying to sell itself as a winter golf destination.

The irreverent Fairway Bill evidently had free rein to write what he pleased in the *Augusta Chronicle*, because he didn't toe the party line, which would have been to pretend the frigid conditions hadn't happened—or at least that they were highly unusual. "It's kind of funny about this Augusta weather," the visitor from Miami wrote, "every time we mention the fact to one of the natives, he'll say, 'Oh, this is most unusual for our town at this time of year.'

"But I notice that all of these native Crackers that were hot footing it over the hills and dales all had their overcoats on, so that shows that their saying on the weather is not in accordance with their apparel."

The column also mentioned that the newspaper men were freezing to death despite the electric heaters provided by the club for their press area on the veranda outside the clubhouse, pointed out that according to the weather report, "We ain't going to get nothing beside North Pole atmosphere tomorrow," and lamented that "it was a tough day on those gallery goddesses, who like to come out to a big event such as this with their new Easter suits, short sleeves, stockingless feet, painted toe nails, eyebrows, and fingernails."

The size of the gallery was undoubtedly affected by the weather and by Jones's position so far back in the field. Club officials said that approximately 700 daily tickets were sold in addition to those already holding series badges, a disappointing number. But there were still a lot of people who wanted to watch Jones, whatever the score, and there was the added bonus of his pairing with Hagen. It was the first time these two great rivals of the 1920s, who accounted for thirteen U.S. and British Opens between them, had played together in a tournament in nine years. So while the crowd was not as large as it might have been, there were still about a thousand spectators following the featured twosome.

Jones and Hagen went off at 10:42 AM, with a vacant "starter's time" before and after them on the tee sheet in recognition of the large gallery that might otherwise bother the pairings ahead and behind. The leaders were nearly all scheduled for the afternoon, pacesetter Horton Smith going off with Denny Shute at 2:15 and Ed Dudley and Billy Burke, tied for second, paired together at 1:26.

Hagen could not be counted out at this stage, just five strokes off the lead, though Jones would need a near miracle at eight behind. Hagen had sounded an optimistic note the afternoon before, saying, "We got to the top with our putters. Now they say we can't putt. We'll show them. The old guard is still in the front line trenches, taking all the fire. Watch Bobby and myself go over the top tomorrow. We take the offensive from now on."

Grantland Rice, while conceding that the odds against the pair were blistering, wrote, "I have a hunch they will set off some fireworks before Saturday's scroll is finally unrolled."

In a way, he was right. Jones did make six birdies on Saturday, but still managed only a 72. While that score was bettered by only ten players in the third round, it still left him ten strokes behind after 54 holes—and that close only because of a late run. Hagen, meanwhile, shot a 70 that was bettered by only one player and remained five strokes out of the lead, giving him a chance heading into Sunday's final round.

Jones's chances of winning ended early on Saturday. At the third hole, 150 yards over water, he was disturbed while standing over the ball by the whirring of a movie camera, not a newsreel camera but one wielded by an amateur in the gallery. Jones stopped, looked up, and said, "Please don't do that." Returning to business, he hit a terrible tee shot that plopped into the middle of Rae's Creek in front of the green, leading to a double bogey.

Robert G. Nixon of the International News Service wrote that Jones, at least on the front nine, contrasted with the "blithe and care-free" Hagen. "Jones was tense and strained. He chewed his lips as the game buffeted him on that front nine. There was a spot of white in each cheek."

Even with three birdies, Jones was two-over on the front nine before he finally showed his old form in going two-under on the back. "It was as if he realized that the 38 on the front nine had left things hopeless," Nixon wrote, "and so he relaxed and came along to score well."

O. B. Keeler saw it differently. He had watched Jones in more than 200 rounds of competition and wrote, "I fail to recall any round that I could set more definitely to his credit than the third round of the Augusta National, when he stepped out under a cold gray sky, hopelessly away from the lead, and, betrayed from the beginning of the tournament by the most trusted part of his great game, fought his way to a par 72 at last."

Keeler noted that it wasn't Jones's greatest scoring round, nor was it an instance where he came through under pressure to win a tournament. But he appreciated that Jones was under the glare of attention in making what everyone was calling his comeback, didn't want to embarrass himself at his own tournament, and must have had some doubts after his performance in the first two rounds, especially on the greens.

His putting was much improved in the third round, thanks perhaps to an old, rusty putter that a friend had brought from Atlanta on Friday night. It was a relative of Calamity Jane (called Calamity Jane III) that Jones had long ago given to his mother, taken from her golf bag at East Lake for delivery to Bobby.

"The club appeared out of place, along with his other shiny instruments," the *New York Times* report noted. "It was rusty and the shaft was of wood."

Whatever works. Jones had only 30 putts in the third round and holed a 15-footer and a 30-footer for birdies. He did not eliminate the shakes on the short ones, however, missing a two-foot birdie putt on the par-five 11th and a pair of four-footers. His lower putt total was also due to improved chipping. His approach on the short par-four 16th finished less than a foot from the hole, as did his chips on the par-five 17th (giving him a birdie) and the par-four 18th (a par).

Congratulated by his father for his back nine, Jones responded, "Well, I feel a bit better about my game today, whether it means anything or not."

Playing together apparently was good for both Jones and Hagen. Sir Walter kept things loose, as usual, at one point joking that he conceded a one-foot putt to Jones. Hagen scored five birdies, all on holes where Jones also birdied, giving the fans plenty to cheer. The Haig even had a chance to come away with a 69, but his drive on the 18th hole came to rest in a divot hole and he bogeyed. Still, at age forty-one, Hagen was showing that while he was past his prime he wasn't necessarily over the hill.

"If Bob and I only had some of these kids whose nerves are still strong putting for us, we might have had two 67s," Hagen said. "As it was, I told him before we started that we had to outplay these kids up to the pin; I think we did. Bob should easily have had a 68 with any luck. I never saw him hitting the harder shots as well."

The gallery got a little too up close and personal with Jones on the 11th fairway when his shoe came right off his foot after a spectator stepped on his heel—fans walked right along with the players in the fairways in those days. "Don't worry about it," the polite Jones told the overzealous patron. "I'm glad you didn't step on my hand."

Many in the gallery rushed forward to try to get a view as soon as Hagen and Jones played their shots, but *Chronicle* reporter Josh Skinner talked to a preacher and three companions who used the opposite strategy and said they didn't miss a shot. "Just wait for everybody else to run down the fairway, clutter the sides, and scramble hither and thither," the preacher advised "Then all you have to do is get right behind the player and see everything."

Playing in the twosome behind Jones and Hagen were Charlie Yates and another player with an East Lake connection, Errie Ball. The twenty-three-year-old Ball, born in Wales and raised in England, emigrated to the United States in 1930 to become an assistant professional to his uncle, Frank Ball, at East Lake. Errie was encouraged to make the move by Jones, who he met at the 1926 British Open (which he played in as a fifteen-year-old).

Ball, who won the 1931 Southeastern PGA and 1932 Atlanta Open and eventually played in 10 U.S. Opens, by 2011 was the only member of the first Masters field still alive. At the age of 100, he still recalled his excitement at getting his invitation to the first Masters.

"I was surprised and tickled to death," he recalled. "I knew if Bobby Jones had anything to do with it, it would be great."

Ball said that the first Masters felt like an informal affair, not nearly as serious as it later became. He even remembered there being barrels of corn whiskey placed around the course. That's hard to verify, but it's a recollection that has popped up from other sources through the years, too.

Evidence of the informality could be found in pairings such as Yates and Ball, who were good friends, and Jones and Hagen. George Jacobus and Charlie Hall, present and past presidents of the PGA were paired in every round.

On the other hand, one thing seems more formal compared to today— most of the players wore ties when they competed. The era of players taking to the course in neckwear was nearing its end, but with Southern gentleman Jones hosting this wasn't a week the players were going to leave their ties at home. However, it was noted that some players donned trousers instead of wearing the more traditional knickers favored by Jones and many others.

Smith did wear a tie and knickers, and he continued to play well in addition to looking dapper. He lengthened his lead with birdies on three of the first five holes, sinking putts of between eight and 30 feet, but couldn't quite keep that pace. Bogeys on Nos. 9 and 10 set him back, but he chipped close for a birdie on the par-five 11th and parred the last seven holes for a 70.

"I started out getting away with a good deal—some freak shots," Smith told Keeler after the round. "Then I started to run into some retributive justice, and I had to fight hard the rest of the way to hold what I had."

Smith received relatively little space in the newspapers compared to Jones, even with Bobby lagging 10 strokes behind. Others received even less attention, but as things shook out at the end of the day it appeared that the tournament would be fought out between five players who were within three strokes of each other. Smith was at 212 through three rounds, Billy Burke at 213, Craig Wood and Ed Dudley at 214, and Paul Runyan at 215.

All of them bettered par on Saturday, led by Wood with a 69, matching Dudley's record of the day before. Wood owned twelve tour victories at the age of thirty-two, had been a member of the last two U.S. Ryder Cup teams, and led the 1932–33 winter tour in earnings, so he was a serious threat. The upstate New York native was one of the longest hitters in the game, but three of his five birdies in the third round came on par threes.

Burke was right on Smith's heels after rounds of 72-71-70, and he could have taken a share of the lead if not for three-putting the 18th hole. Of Lithuanian descent, the thirty-one-year-old was born in Connecticut with the name Burkauskus. A burly fellow who seemed to constantly be smoking a cigar, Burke came from a blue-collar background and had lost part of the fourth finger of his left hand while laboring as an iron worker.

Burke's greatest claim to fame was a victory in the 1931 U.S. Open at Inverness in Ohio where he had to go 144 holes to beat George Von Elm, two 36-hole playoffs being necessary to decide it, and then only by a margin of one stroke (after that, the USGA reverted to 18-hole playoffs). He reportedly went through thirty-two cigars in the course of the championship. Asked how the players withstood the physical test of playing so many rounds in the heat, Burke said, "George Von Elm lost fifteen pounds." What about you, Billy? "I gained three."

Home pro Dudley followed his second-round 69 with a 71 but, like Burke, three-putted the final hole. Runyan continued his comeback from his disappointing 74 on Thursday as he followed his second-round 71 with a 70 on Saturday.

It was two strokes from Runyan to the next players, Hagen and Willie Macfarlane, who were five strokes back at 217 after shooting 70s Saturday but would need a real charge to have a chance on Sunday. Macfarlane and Macdonald Smith both grew up in Scotland and observed to a reporter in the morning that the cold, foggy conditions made them feel right at home.

Mac Smith, however, slipped to a 74 and was six strokes back at 218, his chances of a win at forty-four dwindling. Macfarlane was forty-three, but, curiously, was in his tournament prime. When he was in his twenties and thirties he didn't really like to play tournaments, though he made occasional appearances and won the 1925 U.S. Open in a playoff over Jones. But after turning forty in 1930, he decided to play more regularly. The slim man whose rimless glasses made him look like a schoolmaster compiled fifteen wins in his forties, a figure topped in PGA Tour history by only Vijay Singh and Sam Snead.

The weather didn't make club officials happy, the *Chronicle's* Tom Wall noting that it dampened their enthusiasm. But Fairway Bill, after his rant about the weather, must have felt like making it up to the tournament organizers.

"Never has it been my pleasure to work with so many wonderful appreciative golfers, all with one thought in mind, the Augusta National must go over," he wrote.

The course *was* going over quite well—but would it be enough to attract more members in the midst of the Depression?

The weather was even worse on Sunday, when the high temperature was just 47 degrees. Hardy spectators bundled up in overcoats and hats, and players scrambled to find the warmest clothes they had packed. It's a good thing for Augusta that there was no television in those days: Seeing players blowing on their hands to keep warm and fans dressed like they were going to a Big Ten football game in November wouldn't have been a good advertisement for the city as a warm winter destination.

Some of the contenders went off early, the idea being that it would give the gallery a chance to come out early and walk around with a good pairing and still have a chance to see another feature pair. It also gave these players—Wood, Burke, and Dudley—a chance to post a good number on the scoreboard for later starters Smith and Runyan to see, and possibly fret over.

Wood was the first contender off the tee, and he got off to a rousing start with a phenomenal recovery shot on the first hole. He blocked his tee shot deep into the woods on the right, and his second shot hit a tree and ricocheted even farther back into the grove.

"Well, there he goes out of the tournament," a spectator was heard to say. "And I'd just laid a bet on him."

Bob Harlow in *PGA Magazine* wrote that "it looked impossible to reach the green. It was like playing a ball through a jungle and hoping it would miss everything. There were tall pine trees with huge trunks; dogwood, magnolia, oaks and holly trees and small bushes. There was not even an opening back to the fairway."

It appeared Wood would have to go backward into the adjacent ninth fairway, but he either saw a small opening nobody else did or decided to hit and hope. He took out an eight-iron and his shot somehow made it through the trees, hit on the embankment above the green, rolled down, and ended up an inch from the hole. "The crowd gasped in astonishment and then burst into a cheer," Harlow wrote. "It was more than a million to one. You can go out there and play shots from that spot until you are too old to any longer swing the club and never get one ball as close to the hole as Wood's ball."

Instead of a double bogey, triple bogey, or worse, Wood walked away with a miraculous par. If he had gone on to win the tournament, it would have been a shot for the ages. Instead, the Masters produced a shot for the ages the very next year—with Wood as the victim.

Wood parlayed his great escape into an eventual round of 71, with two birdies against a lone bogey, a fine score under the frigid conditions and a three-under 285 total that was sure to get the attention of the leaders.

"Craig Wood's score was posted. He could not lose a stroke anywhere," Keeler wrote. "And there were seven thousand places, and then some, on that great course where the quartet of pursuers could lose a stroke, or more."

Burke and Dudley came next, paired for the second straight day. If Dudley had a home-course advantage, it didn't show as he shot a lackluster 74 that dropped him to 288 and ultimately a fifth-place finish as the names of the top five remained the same from the third to the fourth round. The Georgia native would finish in the top six of the Masters six times between 1934 and 1941 but never win it. Those accounted for a quarter of his career twenty-four top-ten finishes in majors without a victory.

Burke made a valiant bid for his first victory since 1932 as he tried to regain the form that won him a U.S. Open. The straight hitter from Connecticut found most of the fairways and gave himself birdie chances, but couldn't convert enough of them on what became a day of frustration, especially toward the end.

His birdie putts on the last three holes stopped on the lip of the cup without dropping. The last two, a 10-footer on the 17th and a 20-footer on the 18th, seemed to defy gravity as they tottered on the edge of the hole but refused to fall.

"The crowd each time yelled for him to wait for a breeze to blow the ball in," the *New York Times* reported. "Each time the ball seemed to be looking down into the cup. There was a wind blowing, but it never seemed to strike the ball. Each time Burke was forced to tap the ball in."

He ended up with an agonizing 73 for a total of 286, one behind the score posted by Wood and two behind the ultimate winning score. He could only lament what might have been.

Runyan's bid ended early on two holes of what is now known as Amen Corner, though in this year they were played as part of the front nine. He bogeyed the par-three third hole after hitting his tee shot into a bunker, then drowned his chances with a double bogey on the par-five fourth. He hit his drive into the creek on the left, was able to blast out into the fairway from a muddy spot, but proceeded to hit his fairway-wood third shot into the creek short of the green.

Runyan recovered admirably to play the last 14 holes in four-under for a 71 that landed him in a third-place tie with Burke. Slow starts to the tournament and final round were too much to overcome, but in the end the little man from Arkansas justified his position as one of the best players in the game.

He also played a role in Smith's run at victory by lending him an extra driver that Horton had noticed the day before the tournament.

"Preceding the Augusta competition, I experienced some difficulty with drives, due to hitting downward too much and harder than necessary, thus tensing the swing and destroying freedom," Smith later wrote in a magazine article. "I discovered a driver in Paul Runyan's possession which I thought could help remedy this fault. It had a very deep face which provided enough hitting surface to permit teeing the ball higher, so that I could swing it off cleanly without feeling that I should hit down at it."

The driver also had a springy shaft that eliminated Smith's tendency to try to swing too hard.

Improved driving landed Smith the lead through 54 holes, but holding it wouldn't be easy. He had been in the pressure cooker for the entire tournament, tied for the lead after the first round and a stroke ahead after the second and third—not far enough ahead to have a real cushion but just enough to have a target on his back. The drought of victories in recent years must have also be weighing on his mind as he came down the stretch of such a big tournament.

"Everyone was terribly keen to win. There was a tensity that I don't recall seeing at any previous championship," Smith acknowledged. But he held up by using what was essentially a psychological trick.

"Frankly, I did not expect to win and had managed to convince myself that inasmuch as I had not accepted the responsibility of winning, I need not be upset at any bad developments so long as I used good judgment and played shots to the best of my knowledge and ability."

Smith was even par through eight holes, with a bogey on the par-three third where his tee shot found a bunker and a birdie on the par-five sixth where his 25-foot eagle putt hit the hole and stayed out. His second shot on the ninth found a bunker, giving Horton a "here we go again" feeling since he had bogeyed the hole in the last two rounds. His explosion shot left him a downhill, 15-foot putt for par. When the ball found the hole, it gave him a surge of confidence.

Wood had finished his round while Smith was on the front nine, so the man they were now calling "the Joplin Pine" or "the Oak from Oak Park" knew he needed an even-par 36 on the back nine for the victory. It was not an easy task, especially under the frigid conditions. He immediately gave himself a cushion by holing another 15-footer on the 10th hole, this one for a birdie.

Smith bogeyed the 440-yard par-four 14th, the toughest hole on the course, when he missed the green, hit a chip shot fairly close, but missed the putt. It appeared his nerves were starting to fray when he then three-putted for a bogey on the par-three 15th, missing from three-and-a-half feet. Now he was one-over for the round and needed to play the last three holes in one-under to beat Wood or at even par to tie and force a playoff.

This was a test of Smith's unflappable nature. He was known for not letting things bother him, but that was when he was a young player on an unprecedented roll. Now he was a veteran who had accumulated some scar tissue, facing a situation he had never dealt with before in such an important tournament.

Smith steadied himself and parred the 16th. The uphill, 500-yard par-five 17th offered a birdie opportunity. Smith hit a straight drive, but not long enough to get home in two so he played his second shot to the right and short of the green to leave a better angle for his pitch shot. It went a little farther right than he wanted, leaving him with a 75-yard third shot.

The pitch was a fairly good one, but it checked up quickly and stopped 10 feet short. The gallery hushed as Smith lined up the putt that would give him the lead. He knocked it in the center of the hole.

Smith handled the 18th hole flawlessly on the first two shots, splitting the fairway with his drive and hitting the green with his second, some 25 feet past the flag as he made sure to clear the front bunker. But he left his downhill putt three-and-a-half feet short—the same distance he missed from on 15. He stepped up and sank it to become the first Masters champion.

"I feel that I am back on my game after three years of trying," said Smith, who credited his driving for the victory, though his putting touch on Augusta National's treacherous greens was undoubtedly a factor.

Keeler called Smith's final round "a singularly gallant and conclusive display of golfing merit, intelligence, and sheer courage."

Over 72 holes, he had put together a remarkably consistent performance. He shot 70-72—142 on the first 36 holes and 70-72—142 on the last 36, and also totaled 142 on both the front nine (36-36-34-36) and back nine (34-36-36-36).

There was no green jacket ceremony for the winner; that didn't start until 1949. (It was in the late 1930s that members started wearing green jackets, the original idea being to be able identify them in case tournament patrons had any questions.) Instead, Smith was handed the $1,500 winner's check by Jones himself, which was like being recognized by royalty.

There was a wait for the ceremony. The leader didn't go off last in those days, and there were still thirteen twosomes on the course when Smith finished, but no players with a real chance to win.

Jones himself was still on the course when Smith completed play, having teed off thirty-five minutes later. The Emperor was still king to the galleries, as again about a thousand people followed him (paired with Hagen again) even with the tournament being decided elsewhere. In fact, when Jones was walking down the second fairway he siphoned off a good portion of what was originally a sizable gallery following Smith, who was just completing the nearby fifth hole.

As he had done on Saturday, Jones put on a good show, making five birdies in a round of even-par 72. Remarkably, Jones had more subpar holes for the tournament than Smith, making seventeen birdies while Smith was notching fifteen birdies and an eagle. But Jones finished 10 strokes behind, and six-over par, because he made seventeen bogeys and three double bogeys compared to thirteen bogeys and no doubles for Smith. Many of those over-par figures, of course, were due to missed short putts.

Jones had a pair of three-putts on Sunday, but using the same rusty putter as the day before he again managed to hole a few putts as well, including a 40-footer for a birdie on the seventh. After finding the water and making a bogey on the par-five fourth, he played the last 14 holes in three-under. Now *this* was the Jones the people came out to see.

The fast finish lifted Jones to a tie for 13th place with Hagen, who had a disappointing 77 in the final round, and Denny Shute. It was his worst finish ever in open competition against the pros, rivaled only by an 11th at the 1927 U.S. Open. Since the top twelve players were paid, he finished just barely out of the money, which spared any mention of him receiving or not receiving prize money.

As much a friend as a reporter, Keeler wrote this about Jones: "I may say now very frankly that I never at any time expected Bobby to win this tournament. After his calamitous start, I was wondering what indeed might befall him. And his performance, whatever he may think of it, and whatever the public—never too discerning—may think of it, has made me very happy." He pointed out that a tie with Hagen and the holder of the British Open title—Shute—wasn't too bad after four years away from competition.

Rumors circulated that Jones would play in the U.S. Open that summer. Asked about it by Keeler, Jones responded, "Nerts!" which is to say an emphatic no.

His other writer friend, Rice, asked Jones if he'd had fun. "Not a bit this time," Bobby answered. "When you hit your drives and approaches and all your harder shots and can't putt, you suffer, no matter what your handicap. It is the worst suffering in golf."

But Jones gave a more expansive view to the Associated Press: "I would have enjoyed myself more if I had got more of my short putts down but I had a good time, anyway, and I hope the rest of the fellows did."

Also finishing ahead of Jones were Macfarlane at 291; Harold McSpaden, Jimmy Hines, Al Espinosa, and Macdonald Smith at 292; and Mortie Dutra and Al Watrous at 293.

The twenty-five-year-old McSpaden birdied the first four holes of the final round and shot a 69. That tied the course record of Dudley and Wood, but the fact that nobody could do better than three-under in any round was an indication of what a challenge the course posed. Some very good players posted some big numbers: Leo Diegel, Johnny

Revolta, and Ky Laffoon (a four-time winner in 1934) finished at 296; Bobby Cruickshank at 300; Joe Turnesa at 306; Johnny Farrell at 307; and Harry Cooper, Bill Mehlhorn, and Wiffy Cox withdrew after 54 holes, with an average score among them of 77 (there was no 36-hole cut).

Ball saw just how tough the course was—or, more specifically, how tough the greens were. "The sloping, fast greens were the course's main defense," he remembered much later. "I had never seen anything like them."

In 23rd place after rounds of 74-77-75, Ball hit his tee shot to 10 feet on the par-three third on Sunday—and froze over the ball. He couldn't hit the putt for the longest time, and when he finally did it was an uncontrolled jab that sent the ball farther past the hole than he started from. He took four putts, made a double bogey, and was a basket case for the rest of the round, shooting an 86.

"I developed the yips from it," Ball said. "We called them the twitches in England. It took me a good eight years to get over that."

Yates, playing with Ball again, didn't let his friend's woes affect him, shooting a 72 in the final round to earn low amateur honors and a tie for 21st at 297, proving he belonged in the field. Yates went on to win the British Amateur in 1938 and finish as low amateur in the Masters five times. He became a member at Augusta National in 1940.

In 2001, Yates looked back at playing in the first Masters. "It had a definite feel," he said. "This [what the Masters became] is just a continuation of what they had been doing. The way Bob and Cliff [Roberts] worked to make the tournament the success it was, I knew it was going to be better and better all the time."

On Sunday evening came word that the Masters would be back next year, with plans to make it an annual event.

"I am agreeably surprised at the interest displayed in our tournament and I am inclined to think that we have inaugurated a meeting of golfers and the golfing fraternity generally that should be made a winter feature," Jones said in an official statement.

More colloquially, he told reporters, "Unless I break down completely, I will play in this tournament in 1935. . . . I hope to participate annually, regardless of where I finish."

# 11

## 1934 POST-MASTERS/ STAYING ALIVE

**A**UGUSTA NATIONAL DIDN'T RELEASE attendance figures (a policy that continues to this day), but on the Monday after the tournament Augusta Mayor Thomas Barrett said that total attendance for four days was 15,000.

Recall that when Fielding Wallace was asking for the city to appropriate money to help run the tournament, he cited Grantland Rice's estimate that the Masters would draw 20,000 visitors from out of town. Most of those presumably would have been on hand for the whole tournament, which would have led to a four-day attendance of about 80,000 (with any subtractions for visitors not attending all four days made up for by ticket sales to local people).

Even the 15,000 attendance figure was undoubtedly an overestimation or exaggeration. David Owen's *The Making of the Masters* reports that total ticket sales amounted to $8,011. It depends how that was divided up among $5 (plus tax) series badges good for the whole tournament, $2 daily tickets, and $1 practice round tickets, but no matter how you slice it that translates to a total paid attendance for the four tournament days of no more than 5,000. That's in line with estimates of the crowd following Jones being about a thousand each day, given that such numbers are themselves usually overestimates and that the bulk of the crowd followed him. It's possible the number of people on hand was swelled somewhat, but not to a major degree, by tickets being given away or people sneaking onto the grounds.

There were no complaints about falling short of pre-tournament estimates from the cheerleaders at the *Augusta Chronicle*, who seemed to promptly forget about the 20,000-visitor pie-in-the-sky projection it had incessantly trumpeted. In a post-tournament editorial, the Masters was called "the biggest golfing event ever held in the South" and a report on the commercial impact of the tournament stated that "the visitors to the city during the past week have been as numerous as expected" even while mentioning that there was not a shortage of accommodations at any of the hotels.

Still attendance at the Masters was in line with most tournaments of the time, so the tournament was reasonably successful in that regard. The attendance wasn't as big as a U.S. Open, but that championship was generally played in larger cities with gate receipts in mind.

The *Chronicle* also reported on the Tuesday after the tournament that there was a "strong likelihood" the U.S. Open would be held at Augusta National in 1935, citing an unnamed member of the club as its source. The Open and the Masters would reportedly both be held in March 1935. That, of course, didn't happen. The USGA officials who attended the Masters were undoubtedly impressed with the course, but they were not ready to move the U.S. Open to March.

The 1934 Masters finished in the black, according to Clifford Roberts at the time, but if you consider course improvements to be part of tournament expenses the club lost money on it. The club spent the bulk of the city's $10,000 on course work, plus tournament infrastructure like scoreboards and tents. When it came time to pay the purse of $5,000, Clifford Roberts had to ask members to make up for a short-fall; without those individual contributions he wouldn't have been able to make a full payout to the players. A member named Bart Arkell put up first prize and Jay Monroe covered second-place money.

The Masters did help to drum up new members, according to Owen in *The Making of the Masters.* Just a couple weeks after the tournament, Roberts mentioned in a letter to Alister MacKenzie's widow, Hilda, that the club had gained eighteen or twenty new members, giving it "a better chance of being a success."

The inflow of initiation fees and dues helped the club to maintain operations for the next year, though the long-term future was still anything but assured.

From the city's perspective, the best thing about the Masters was the publicity. The comeback of Bobby Jones had attracted writers who pounded out so much copy that the Masters topped the U.S. Open in telegraph transmissions. Wire service stories on the tournament were displayed prominently in newspapers across the country.

It was pointed out that if you had to pay for this kind of advertising, it would have cost far more than the $10,000 the city laid out for the tournament. That's true, but it remained to be seen how *effective* that advertising would be, whether it would pay off in significantly increased tourist visits to Augusta and revenue for the city.

The importance of Jones to the tournament was clear from Rice's follow-up story on the Masters in the May 1934 issue of the *American Golfer.* "The Augusta National's annual Masters' Tournament is on its way to become one of the big fixtures in golf, presenting Bobby Jones again next spring in his second start since 1930," he wrote in the first paragraph.

The Masters didn't become one of the three biggest tournaments on tour in 1934 (along with the U.S. Open and PGA Championship) because Jones was *hosting* a tournament. It drew such intense coverage and interest because he was *playing* in a tournament. Without that element, it would likely have been something akin to the La Gorce Open—an event that drew a top field but didn't entice national writers or deliver banner headlines nationwide. And Rice's take on the tournament showed that Jones the player would be the key in 1935, too.

Jones had only agreed to play in the tournament for the sake of keeping his club afloat in tough economic times. However, the nation's writers weren't aware of Augusta National's financial woes, and thus didn't know the real reason Jones had agreed to play. So, naturally, they had their own takes on why Jones "came back" from retirement. Generally, it was assumed he had done so because of a competitive itch that needed to be scratched and a desire to see how he stacked up against the current crop of players.

This assumption led to the speculation that Jones would play in other tournaments besides the Masters. Since his performance at Augusta had shown he was rusty, he naturally would want to play more in order to be able to perform at his best.

"This much we know: that [Jones] has great pride in his golf; that he entered this tournament not only to make the tournament, but to see for himself whether he had slipped," wrote Los Angeles writer Darsie L. Darsie. "The fact that his long game is good, but his putting is bad will lead him to believe that he has not slipped—and it will be surprising if Bobby doesn't decide to take a fling at the national open this year when it is played in Philadelphia."

Jones had no desire to play in any more U.S. Opens. From his writings, one gets the sense that Bobby didn't really *enjoy* competition. That's probably a big reason why he retired. He had been perfectly content to stay away from competitive golf for the rest of his life until circumstances forced him to make an exception.

Clearly, the long absence from competition took its toll and was the main reason Jones wasn't a factor in the tournament, despite practice-round scores that would have put him right in there with a chance to win if he had been able to reproduce them.

"Until the tournament began, I did not realize what a big difference there is between playing these friendly practice rounds and a tournament where every shot counts," he said after the tournament. "I simply could not get putting confidence and control, no matter how much advice or how many clubs I tried."

The thoughtful, analytical Horton Smith offered an explanation when a reporter approached him in the lobby of the Bon Air after the second round and asked why Jones had lost his touch.

"My idea of it is something like this," Smith replied. "A fellow loses the vital part of his game without realizing it. It is sort of a spiritual quality which one's game develops in competition. Jones has been playing friendly rounds for four years. He has been getting along playing easily and knowing that nothing mattered. If he missed a shot, he didn't worry about it. There was no iron in his game. Because there didn't have to be any.

"The reason I say it is sort of a spiritual quality is because it becomes sort of a mental code to adhere to. It builds up something in the subconscious mind. It is something that can be called on in an emergency. You read about competitive athletes calling upon some hidden wells of strength. I think it is that iron in the mind which only continued competition builds up.

"Now Jones hasn't had a match that required any of this iron will. He played well enough in those friendly rounds. But suddenly he comes back to competition. He finds that the game that matters is different from the one which doesn't."

Jones no doubt wasn't happy that he was considered the favorite to win the tournament. But with all eyes on him, he wanted to make sure that he put his best foot forward, that he was as prepared as he could be. So he put in a lot of practice in the weeks leading up to the tournament—and was playing so well that even he might have thought, "Hey, maybe I *can* win this thing."

Rice thought that Jones might have played too much in the two weeks leading into the tournament and was mentally stale by the time the bell rang. Besides that, his duties as host were an additional burden that may have prevented him from playing his best.

In any case, Jones saw a bright side after it was all over. "I am glad that this idea of invincibility in golf is shattered," he told Rice. "The game of golf still dominates the player, and there is no one even close to being a superman. I know I am not."

Had the proof that he wasn't a superman removed a bit of the shine from the Jones legend? That was a risk he took by putting himself out there in competition again. The pros were shooting scores week in and week out that were better than those Jones had produced in the 1920s. This was mostly due to the introduction of steel shafts, but still if Bobby didn't do well it would give people a chance to say that he just couldn't keep pace with the current crop of low-scoring pros. That proved to be a minority view, even after his lackluster showing. The fact that Jones struck the ball so well from tee to green in the Masters helped to preserve his reputation as a great player, though one who had succumbed to the putting woes that had afflicted other greats, such as Harry Vardon, when they got older. The only difference was that for thirty-two-year-old Jones it was more the layoff than it was his age.

In retrospect, Jones's showing wasn't really a surprise, even to those who figured beforehand Jones would ride in and be as great as ever. Syndicated columnist Joe Williams put it this way: "Jones spotted the field a tremendous advantage the chief of which, I still maintain, is a basic one, applicable to all competitive sports—which is, to repeat, that when you quit it is almost impossible to come back."

As for the tournament itself, it was a benefit for Augusta National to have as a member the nation's most famous sports writer and editor of the *American Golfer*. Rice wrote in that magazine that the first Masters was "an amazing success" and that "I have rarely seen any gallery more keyed up for four days than this invasion from thirty-eight states, Canada, and England, happened to be. The crowds by early spring dusk were limp from excitement and over-worked nerves."

A couple months after the Masters, Horton Smith was asked what he thought of it. "It was one of the greatest tournaments I ever played in," he replied. "I have never found such tremendous interest as there was in this Augusta event. Bobby made the tournament. And to get an idea of how popular this Georgia chap is, one pro, who has never been very friendly to Jones, said after it was all over, 'That Jones is a wonder. I think more of him now than I ever thought it was possible for me to think of anyone. The way he handled himself made me an admirer of his for life.'"

And what of Jones's ideal course, Augusta National? It drew surprisingly little comment, considering it was the debut of what would go on to become the most famous course in America.

But aside from some complaints about pin positions, the returns were positive. "There is nothing monotonous about that course and it is one of the most beautiful I ever played," said Smith. "Each one of the holes presents something new."

In analyzing the scoring results, Jones was pleased with the way the course played. The fact that Smith didn't make a double bogey, Jones wrote in a preview of the 1935 Masters in the *American Golfer*, showed that the course played as intended. "In the beginning it was decided that severe penalties for one wayward shot should, so far as possible, be eschewed. . . . It was intended to be a course which would keep taking a toll of a stroke here and there from the erring player, but upon which one was not likely to run into disaster on any one hole."

Jones was also happy that the average score of the top twenty-four players was comfortably under par on all of the par fives, ranging from 4.552 on the sixth (today's 15th) to 4.875 on the fourth (today's 13th). "I think the most deadly, boring holes on a golf course are those prodigious affairs which can be reached with three ordinary shots but never with two excellent ones. I think a par five should always be of the kind that can be played as a great par four if the player is man enough to do so. Holes like this give the big hitter a chance to do his stuff."

They also provided excitement for tournament play. Smith played the par fives in 11-under for the tournament, including an eagle on the 17th in the first round and a winning birdie on the same hole on Sunday. And Jones displayed his intact long-game skills and thrilled the galleries with his fairway-wood second shots to the par fives.

But Augusta National extracted a toll on the par fours and par threes, proving to be a course that no one could truly master, with only four players breaking par for 72 holes. The hardest holes were two of the longer par fours, the 440-yard 14th (today's fifth) and 425-yard fifth (today's 14th) both playing to a 4.354 average for the top twenty-four players. As much as length, the difficulty on both holes was caused by a mound at the front of the green that added to the challenge of approach shots and created a dilemma whether to chip, pitch, or putt if the ball came up short of the green.

The uphill 420-yard ninth (today's 18th) at 4.343 was nearly as tough, with the creek-guarded 150-yard third (today's 12th) the most challenging par three at 3.333.

After the tournament Jones analyzed how the course played and decided to make some changes—a practice that has continued through the years. The third green (today's 12th) was rebuilt to improve drainage, a new bunker (since removed) was installed on the second fairway (today's 11th), and four greens were extended at the front.

Two of those greens were the fifth and 14th, the holes that played the toughest. Originally, the mounds on both of these greens were at the very front of the putting surfaces. MacKenzie and Jones intended for those holes to accommodate a run-up approach over the mounds. But Jones observed at the first Masters that the fairways often didn't produce enough bounce and roll for the run-up shot, so he extended the green in front of the mounds to make it easier to bounce the ball in and roll it up and over the mound to the main part of the putting surface.

It was a flaw H.J. Whigham had noted in his otherwise glowing review of the course, calling the original 14th a "curiously bad example of what is known as the run-up type of green" because the climb to the plateau was too steep and the grass on the fairway in front of it not fast enough.

Those changes were made over the summer and early fall when the club was closed. Another change was announced in November—the nines would be reversed from the way they played in the 1934 Masters. This was a reversion to MacKenzie's original plan, and the way we know the course as it has played from 1935 until today.

Clifford Roberts wrote forty years later in *The Story of the Augusta National Golf Club* that the switch was made because the front nine as it played in 1934 was more prone to frost on cold mornings so it made sense to start on the other nine. That reason applied to member play in the heart of the winter. From the standpoint of the tournament the reason for the switch, as stated by the club at the time, was to give the players a chance to play the easier nine first before reaching the "intricate problems of the difficult holes," as the *Chronicle* put it.

It's not that the two nines were that different in difficulty. But the water hazards on the course are nearly all located on the current back nine (on the 11th, 12th, 13th, 15th, and 16th holes). It was felt— apparently a mutual decision by Jones and Roberts—that it would be better for players to face those more severe penalties deep into the round rather than starting on the second hole.

It was a brilliant decision as far as the Masters was concerned.(It could be said it was simply the correction of a bad decision to reverse the nines in the first place.) The back nine holes are ideal for creating tournament excitement, because many of them offer birdie opportunities while also threatening potential disasters. That makes for great leaderboard volatility and exciting action that helped the Masters earn, and keep, its place as the most anticipated and most watched event in golf.

It also put holes like the 12th and 13th into the spotlight—and onto television screens when that medium came along—cementing their reputations as two of the best holes on any course in the world.

# 12

## 1935 PRE-MASTERS/ THE NEXT CHAPTER

**IF MASTERS OFFICIALS MADE** one misstep in the tournament's first year, it was inviting a number of players who didn't belong in an elite field. The Associated Press noticed. Its sports editor, Alan Gould, decided after the inaugural Augusta National event that the wire service would not refer to the event as the Masters because the field didn't justify the name.

Jones had felt pressure from Spalding to invite some of the company's pros, according to Charles Price in *A Golf Story*. But Gould wasn't troubled by the presence of journeyman tour pros as much as he was by players like two Englishmen he had never heard of—C.T. Wilson, who shot 80-83-80-79 and C.G. Stevens, who withdrew after shooting 81-82.

Jones and Roberts were aware of the criticism and moved to correct matters by setting criteria upon which they would base invitations. The announced standards were:

1. Past and present U.S. Open champions

2. Past and present U.S. Amateur champions
3. Past and present British Open champions
4. Past and present British Amateur champions
5. Present members of the Ryder Cup team
6. Present members of the Walker Cup team
7. The first twenty-four players in the first Augusta National Invitation Tournament

Note: Other players selected on the basis of past competitive records; particular consideration being given to scoring averages established in various leading tournaments in 1934.

This was better, though the last part was vague enough that it still pretty much allowed Augusta to invite whoever it wanted. The Associated Press stuck with its edict of calling it the Augusta National Golf Club's invitation tournament instead of the Masters. This might have pleased Jones, because it was the name he wanted the tournament to be known as, but he wouldn't have been happy about the reason.

Under the new guidelines, 138 players were invited. That's a large number, but since all living past U.S. and British Open and Amateur champions were on the official invitation list, it included a lot of players who certainly weren't going to play, especially those on the other side of the Atlantic.

Augusta National released the names of all the 1935 invitees, something it didn't do in 1934. There were ninety-three Americans, thirty-four from Great Britain, four Canadians, three each from France and Japan, and one from Argentina. Again, the international invitees were largely token. Not a single player from any other country than Canada made the journey to Augusta, and only two of the four Canadians did. England's Henry Cotton, the 1934 British Open champion, indicated in December that he would play, but at the end of January said he wouldn't be able to make it.

A look at the list of invited Americans shows that Augusta National was liberal in interpreting "other players on the basis of past competitive records." Ninety-three was a large number for what was supposed to be an elite tournament, and the list included a few pros who are not remembered today and whose names probably didn't resonate even then. On top of that, Augusta made an agreement with the PGA to invite the top five players from the winter tour not already on the list. PGA tournament manager Robert Harlow told his players that made Augusta practically an open tournament instead of an invitational, since nearly all of the winter tour regulars were already invited. (Remember, there were far fewer tour regulars than there are today). And the invitation list was swelled by thirty-five amateurs.

Still, it all worked out pretty well in the end. Most of the amateurs and a few of the obscure or old-time pros didn't come. Traveling a long way to Augusta as an amateur, or even as a professional unlikely to earn a check by finishing in the top twelve, must have been cost prohibitive for many. So the field wasn't littered with no-names, and this time nearly all of the best players *did* accept the invitation.

Of the top twenty-five players from the 1934 tour, only two did not play in the 1935 Masters: Californian Willie Hunter, who elected not to make the cross-country trip, and Ralph Guldahl, a fine young player from Dallas who would go on to finish second, second, and first in the Masters starting with his 1937 debut appearance. Other name pros missing were Macdonald Smith and Joe Kirkwood, while amateurs invited but not playing included Johnny Goodman and Francis Ouimet. The top fifteen pros from the winter tour of 1934-35 were all present and accounted for.

Even before invitations went out on February 21 some of the prominent players who didn't play in 1934 assured Augusta officials they would tee it up this time—Tommy Armour gave word in December, Olin Dutra in January, and Gene Sarazen in early February.

"All of the 'big shots' are talking of the tournament," Augusta National pro Ed Dudley said after playing in the Miami Biltmore Open in December.

That showed the tournament was continuing to move forward after a positive start. The Masters and the city of Augusta also got good news with greatly improved rail service, which included a better overnight schedule to New York and new overnight service from Florida. The latter was important because the hope was that the Masters would induce some of the Sunshine State's winter residents to stop in Augusta on their way back to the Northeast. That's one reason the 1935 Masters moved back a couple weeks, scheduled for April 4 to 7. It was also timed to coincide with the end of baseball spring training to make it convenient for sports writers heading north.

But financially things weren't going so well that Augusta National was ready to go it alone in running the Masters. Once again, it asked the city for money. The club couldn't count on as much the influence from the mayor's office, since Thomas Barrett had died in June of hypertension at the age of forty after little more than five months in office. The city council did approve funding for the Masters, but just $7,500 this time.

Only $5,000 entered the club's coffers. The unpaid water bill from 1933 that was carried forward by the city still hadn't been paid, so $2,500 went as a credit to take care of those charges.

With city money being spent, there was a vocal faction in town that felt the club needed to invite a local player to the Masters (Augusta National pro Ed Dudley didn't count in their eyes since he was a newcomer to the city). Roberts said that he was willing to add an Augusta player, but left it up to Mayor Richard Allen to make that request if he felt it would benefit the tournament. Another faction lobbied Allen *not* to ask that an Augusta player be included, feeling that it was more beneficial for the tournament to build its reputation as a tournament that could truly be called the Masters. The latter group won out, and no local was added to the field.

Roberts's flexibility on the question of inviting an Augusta player indicates how much the tournament still needed the support of the city; his way of handling it so that ultimately it didn't happen shows his ingenuity. This was just one headache for Roberts, who arrived in Augusta on November 30 and stayed through the Masters next spring.

In truth, tournament affairs must have been a pleasure compared to club business. At least the tournament was a successful operation; the club itself was in deep trouble. It had managed to settle the unpaid water bill, but other creditors were lining up with their hands out.

The new memberships from 1934 had helped the club pay its operating costs, but not what it already owed. Various contractors still had not been fully paid from course construction, the club couldn't meet its mortgage payments, and Roberts was trying to hold everyone off as best he could. Some creditors were going to court, and Augusta National lost a suit filed by the McWane Cast Iron Pipe Company over its debt of $1,500.

A week-long quail hunting trip with Jones to Albany, Georgia, in mid-January must have been a welcome diversion for Roberts, but not one on which business could be ignored. Indeed, it must have been arranged as a way to get together to discuss tournament plans.

Jones made visits to Augusta, too, but those were more for the purpose of preparing himself as a player. It's hard to say what he thought of his chances in the tournament, but he surely wanted to do his best, whatever that might be.

The press and public were eager to jump back on the Jones bandwagon. True, he hadn't performed like the Jones of old in the first Masters. But that was just one tournament. Maybe it would be different this time—though with just one tournament under his belt since the summer of 1930 he would be just as ill-prepared for competition as he had been the year before. Still, he was Bobby Jones, and wasn't to be dismissed lightly.

"Golf writers the country over have been dipping their pens in ink wells and writing to the world that the greatest golfer of all time must be taken seriously in this year's tournament," Tom Wall wrote in the *Chronicle*. "He has regained much of the putting mastery which carried him to a pinnacle only Georgia's Jones knows and, since putting was the only department in which he faltered in the initial tournament, critics are inclined to believe now that his greens game has improved, that he will finish among the top one-to-three boys, with the number one position his probable station."

After Jones played Augusta National on March 15, the *Chronicle* talked to his "admiring friends," who relayed the information that Jones had made six putts of 10 to 15 feet. What's more, those friends reported Jones as saying, "It's the first time in four years that I feel like I can walk right up to the ball and make it do what I want it to. I just seem to have more confidence than ever before. I am myself again."

Jones must have had a word with those admiring friends the next day about their loose lips. When asked by a reporter about his putting, Jones replied, "Nice story they had in the paper this morning, but I'm afraid it's a bit premature."

The odds on Jones started at 15 to 1 when they first came out in mid-March, but he received so much backing that within a few days they fell to 11 to 1. By March 31, the Sunday before the tournament, Jones was the favorite at 8 to 1, a role he had all to himself this time.

Grantland Rice was optimistic because he felt that Jones hadn't burned himself out with practice like he had the year before. Even though he was not scoring quite as well (between 70 and 74 this time) in his practice rounds, Rice felt that he would benefit from being fresher come tournament time.

"He confided in me that he would like to get in one fine round to get his confidence back, but he is still hitting the ball with the same free, smooth swing that carried him so high and so far up through 1930," Rice wrote in his syndicated column.

Tommy Armour felt so strongly about Jones that he felt Bobby's odds should be 5 to 1. "He is the type that can get hot on a moment's notice and burn up the course," he told Rice. "Just watch that swing, and we all know he can stand all the pressure there is. What about one tournament competition in five years? That may hurt or it may help."

O.B. Keeler, the man closest to Jones, was more cautious. "They're all agog about Bobby's chances this year," he wrote. "And I really think he will be somewhat better this spring than last. But whether that is good enough, with the wolves on him—I don't know. Nobody knows. But you can't keep them from guessing."

Gould fell off Jones's bandwagon after watching him in a practice round on Monday of tournament week. The Associated Press sports editor wrote that "candor compels the assertion that there's no sound basis for backing the chances of the former king of the golfing realm."

Jones played only nine holes that day and then headed for the practice range to try to figure out what he was doing wrong. "I've been hitting the ball fairly well at times, but I simply need a lot of hard work," Jones said. "I do think I'm putting better—with a replica of my old 'Calamity Jane' except that it's quite a bit heavier—but it's difficult to recapture the old confidence."

Sarazen was the sensation of the practice rounds, shooting 65-72-67-67 for a 271 total in his four rounds before playing in alternate-shot foursomes on Wednesday. To give you an idea how good that was, that's a 72-hole total nobody matched in the tournament proper until Jack Nicklaus in 1965, followed only by Raymond Floyd in

161

1976.Nobody bettered it until Tiger Woods in 1997. Of course, these were just practice rounds, away from the heat of competition, with pins not in the toughest locations, and in his 65 he didn't play from the back of the tees. Nonetheless, Sarazen served notice.

Rice played with Sarazen in two of those practice rounds (members were allowed to play the course except on tournament days), including the 65. "I am hitting the ball better than I have in two years," Sarazen confided to him.

Gene didn't play in the tournaments leading up to the Masters, arriving in Augusta and familiarizing himself with the course he didn't play in 1934. Sarazen wanted to be ready because he considered this a very important tournament and considered Jones a friend. He very much regretted not having been able to play in the first Masters, even though his absence was due to circumstances beyond his control.

"Sarazen has been training like two pro football teams and a brace of major league camps," Rice wrote.

"I'm keen about the course and I never saw any golf battlefield in better shape," Sarazen said. "I honestly think I can step along here."

Sarazen even felt he had luck on his side. At his hotel before the start of the tournament, he ran into an old friend, Bob Davis. Upon shaking hands, Sarazen felt a huge ring on Davis's finer.

"Are you wearing brass knuckles?" Sarazen asked, pulling his hand away.

"Sorry, Gene, but I forgot the heavy silver ring on my third finger," Davis replied.

"Who made it; some blacksmith?" Sarazen asked.

"A souvenir from Mexico. The maker passed from this life more than a century ago. Concerning its history, if you care to listen . . . ?"

Davis then related a tale about the ring having belonged to Benito Juarez, the president of Mexico who overcame French occupation in the 1860s, and made a connection to Sarazen's Italian heritage by

pointing out that Benito Mussolini was named for Juarez, a fact Davis
had learned from Sarazen's father.

"The fact that this ring, once the property of Benito Juarez, linked
vicariously with Benito Mussolini, is now in my possession, convinces
me that destiny has set the stage for a ceremony to be performed, in
the surrender of this ring to your keeping, in the hope that it will
bring you good luck in the four days' competition on the Augusta
National course," Davis proclaimed. "Therefore I place in your
keeping, with all the influence for good that may obtain, this silver
relic once the possession of Benito Juarez."

Davis removed the ring from his finger and presented it to Sarazen.
"That he was impressed is putting it mildly," Davis later related in the
*American Golfer*. Sarazen said that it wouldn't be comfortable to wear
the ring during play, but he would keep it in his pocket.

"Go with confidence down every fairway, Gene. You can't fail,"
Davis said, slapping Sarazen on his back as he walked away.

"Honestly, did that piece of junk ever belong to Juarez?" a friend
asked Davis after Sarazen was gone.

"Absolutely not," Davis answered. "It was made by a modern Mex-
ican silversmith and presented to me by Major Arthur Hamilton
Gibbs last December."

"Well, what's the big idea in loading your friend Sarazen up with
the fake history?"

"An experiment in suggestion. It may work."

The betting public didn't know about the ring, but they were aware
of Sarazen's practice rounds. By Wednesday, Sarazen had become the
betting favorite at 6 to 1, with Jones holding steady at 8 to 1.

Lawson Little was another player people were watching. The
twenty-four-year-old amateur accomplished a sensational double in
1934, winning both the British and U.S. Amateurs, making him yet
another candidate to be the next Bobby Jones. Even the players were

anxious to get a look at the newest sensation up close. For his first practice round, Little was able to find quite a trio of players to join: Jones, Armour, and Walter Hagen.

Little was impressive, especially with his drives. He packed a lot of power on his stocky five-foot-ten frame, and was able to reach the green on the par-five 13th with a drive around the corner and a four-iron. Jones liked what he saw enough to pick Little for his partner in Wednesday's alternate-shot competition.

They teamed for a 72 while playing in the company of winners Olin Dutra and Jimmy Thomson, who shot a 68. The twenty-six-year-old Thomson was just coming into his own on tour. He hadn't won any tournaments yet—he would finish second in the U.S. Open in two months—but had gained a reputation as the longest hitter in the game.

Thomson and Little put on quite a show with what Keeler called their "Homeric swats" off the tee, both hitting first on the odd holes as partners alternated tee shots in the format. Thomson always managed to be at least 10 yards ahead, and on a couple of occasions out-swatted Little by some 40 yards. On the 340-yard seventh hole, each left their partners with an approach of less than 40 yards, prodigious pokes considering the equipment of the day.

Jones wanted to see what Thomson could do on the par-five 13th. After the official tee shots were struck, Jones asked Thomson to go to the back tee (the tee had been set some 15 yards forward that day) and try to hit a drive over the trees that blocked the way at the corner of the dogleg. It was a shot that "nobody had yet been sufficiently psychopathic to try," according to Keeler. "To accomplish this from the rear tee would mean a towering drive that must be at least one hundred feet in the air at a distance of 200 yards, if you can figure that out."

Thomson obliged, taking a mighty swing and sending the ball over the tall trees and the creek into the fairway, leaving just an iron shot in to the green.

This report calls into question, but does not entirely discredit, a story involving Sam Snead. When he was a veteran, he would play with a young player in a practice round and say to him on the 13th tee, "When I was young, I used to drive over those trees and cut the corner." The youngster would try it and watch his ball rattle among the pines, not having attained enough height. "Of course," Snead would add, "when I was young, those trees were a lot shorter,"

Actually, those are old trees and weren't very much shorter when Snead was young. But we shouldn't put it past Snead, a long hitter himself, to have pulled off a Thomsonian feat. Dustin Johnson, incidentally, wowed everyone in 2011 by carrying those trees from a new back tee that has added 30 yards to the hole since Thomson's time— but he had the advantages of a large-headed metal driver and a space-age ball.

Little pronounced himself a fan of Augusta National, both on its own merits and as ideal preparation for his next tournament, the British Amateur (he would repeat the British-U.S. Amateur sweep in 1935).

"It's simply a grand layout. And, speaking a bit selfishly, it's just exactly what I need to get in shape for the British excursion," he said. "I can't think of any other golf course in America that is so ideally calculated to keep a fellow thinking all the time, and hitting the shots as best he can."

Henry Picard, one of the top players of the 1930s, later told his son Larry that the course in those early days was not in the immaculate condition it is today, with some shots having to be played off Georgia red mud or a clover lie. Still, it was in better condition than most courses of the time, and the club worked hard to make sure it was in the best shape possible for the Masters.

Fairway Bill Wallace reported that Alphonse Berckmans "tells me that he was up at five bells yesterday morning, going over the course with a fine-tooth comb, looking for a stray weed, but boss you just know he didn't have a chance to dig one up on that Brussels carpet layout."

About half the field had shortened practice time for the 1935 Masters because they were playing in the Capital City Open in Atlanta, which ended the Monday of Masters week that year because the final 18 holes were delayed a day by rain. Those players were more frazzled than rested due to a hectic schedule which sometimes prevailed in the days when tournaments took less than four days to complete and didn't necessarily end on the weekend.

The North and South Open was played on Wednesday, Thursday, and Friday in Pinehurst, North Carolina. Then, crazy as it sounds, the Capital City Open began the very next day in Atlanta. The 54-hole event originally scheduled the first round on Saturday and final 36 holes on Sunday. Due to a rainstorm, they were only able to get in one round on Sunday.

Players who went straight from Pinehurst to Atlanta, and then on to Augusta, included Picard, Paul Runyan, Harry Cooper, Johnny Revolta, and twenty-three-year-old Byron Nelson, who was making his Masters debut.

The twenty-eight-year-old Picard was just starting to blossom. He came to Augusta fresh off a win in Atlanta—his second victory in three starts and third of the year,—leading the money list with $5,060. Runyan was not to be forgotten after leading the tour in earnings for the second straight year in 1934 while winning the PGA Championship. He hadn't played the whole winter tour, but won the North and

South the week before Augusta and held a narrow lead over Picard in scoring average.

Defending champion Horton Smith had faced more physical woes in 1934, spraining his back again at the U.S. Open and withdrawing from the Western Open shortly afterward because of it. He recovered to post two more victories in 1934, but hadn't broken through yet in 1935.

The Masters was shaping up as a wide-open affair. Following favorites Sarazen and Jones came eight players in a pack at 10 to 1: Picard, Runyan, Smith, Little, Dutra, Dudley, Cooper, and Revolta. Right behind them at 12 to 1 were Thomson, who at the beginning of the week had been dismissed at 50 to 1, and Ky Laffoon, a twenty-five-year-old who had emerged in 1934 with four victories.

The afternoon before the opening round found Jones in a familiar place—on the putting green for an hour trying to figure out how to get the ball in the hole.

"I think I've found something," he declared. "I address the ball as usual, and instead of looking at the back of it, I look at a point two inches ahead and try to hit through that point."

He holed a couple of six-footers, then missed his next three.

"No," he said with a sigh, "I guess I haven't found anything."

# 13

## 1935 ROUNDS 1 AND 2/ THE HERSHEY HURRICANE

**THE PRACTICE ROUNDS WERE** notable for low scoring, Sarazen's sizzling 65 being the most extreme example. But the course wasn't set up to play very tough on the practice days. Maybe things would be different when they played for real.

Not exactly. Four players shot better than the competitive course record of 69 on the tournament's first day and another matched it. Sarazen remained in top form, shooting a 68, as did Atlanta winner Henry Picard, who went one better with a 67 to take the lead. Ray Mangrum and Willie Goggin joined Sarazen at 68, while Craig Wood was at 69.

"Here I had committed my supposedly mature and certainly unbiased judgment to the backing of Old Man Par, against even the unparalleled field assembled for this competition," wrote O.B. Keeler. "And here, at the end of Round 1, is the Old Man back in his corner, bleeding from both gills, and with a busted sacro-iliac from bouncing up after a series of knockdowns."

There were several reasons for the onslaught. The temperature was comfortable. An overnight rain helped to soften the course and take some of the fire out of the greens. The course was in excellent condition and the players were more familiar with it as they tackled it for a second year. A lesser factor in the scoring, but something the players appreciated, was a printed sheet showing the pin positions on the holes where the green was not completely visible on the approach—a novel idea at the time.

Augusta National still wasn't a pushover, with these scores entered as evidence: Tommy Armour and Ed Dudley 73, Bobby Jones, Lawson Little, Horton Smith, Billy Burke, and Jimmy Thomson 74, Harold McSpaden 75, and Ky Laffoon 76.

The most noteworthy of those over-par scores was, of course, that turned in by Jones. His 74 was two strokes better than his opening round of 1934, but this time he was seven strokes behind instead of six.

"I didn't score much better than in the first round last year, but I played a lot better," Jones told Keeler. "For the first time—well, for the first time in years, I felt somewhat comfortable in my shots. Even about the greens, though the putts stayed out pretty consistently. I was hitting my shots better than last year, and had some idea of what I was trying to do. Being out of tournament competition for five years except for this one—well, you know how it is."

Jones's galleries saw how it was on the first hole, where he three-putted for a bogey, a quick indication he wasn't tournament ready. It was one of three three-putts on the day, though he did hole a couple of longish birdie putts. Jones was even par through the first dozen holes, but what really hurt him was the 13th. He hooked his drive into the trees, was able to hit out into the fairway and reach the green in regulation, only to take three putts. A bogey on the 18th, where he missed the green, wasn't a promising finish.

While feeling better about his game, Jones wasn't *too* confident about the coming three rounds. When sports editor Ralph McGill of the *Atlanta Constitution* (the same Ralph McGill who as executive editor in the 1960s would preside over the newspaper's progressive coverage of the Civil Rights struggle) tried to offer some encouraging words about "letting them have it" tomorrow, Jones responded, "Well, I don't know, I have seen them stay this way for a lot of days."

Alan Gould of the Associated Press continued to hammer on the Jones versus the pros angle, writing that the "professional light brigade" was showing Jones and his followers "how it's done nowadays." Jones was "still the choice of the galleries," he noted, "but otherwise no match for the current professional aristocracy." Yet even Gould chose to tell the nation's readers far more about the details of Jones's round than he did about the leaders of the tournament.

Clifford Roberts later wrote that at some point in those early years he sought out Gould and asked him why he didn't devote himself to the good golf being played by some of the competitors instead of the bad golf being played by Jones.

"The reply I received was direct and emphatic," Roberts wrote. "Alan said to me that I should run the tournament and let him write about it. He then stated that, 'There is more news value in a putt missed by Jones than brassie shots being holed out by any other member of the field.'

"I had meant to explain to Alan that Bob's main interest was to establish a golf tournament, and that he deserved the cooperation of his friends in the media. But Alan's blunt remarks knocked the wind out of me for the moment, and I left it until another time to try to enlist his understanding and support."

Apparently, Roberts wasn't yet feeling his oats as tournament chairman—in later years, he surely wouldn't have slinked away without getting in the last word.

Jones was paired with Smith, a twosome of common last names but uncommon drawing power. Last year's winner was in decent shape after making birdies on 15 and 16 to get to one-under, but fell apart on the 17th. His tee shot was pushed to the right and found a road between the 17th and 15th fairways, where his ball settled in a hole. He consulted with Jones, but they couldn't decide whether Smith should get relief, so the match was delayed while word was sent to the clubhouse to fetch an official. Jay R. Monroe, Roberts's second-in-command at the tournament, arrived and ruled that Smith had to play the ball as it lay. Horton came up short of the green with his second, pitched on, and three-putted for a double bogey, which he followed with a bogey on the 18th for his 74. He was left with a daunting task ahead of him to defend his championship.

Picard's 67 could have been even better but he, too, suffered a bogey on the 18th where he hit his approach into the right bunker and his par putt hung on the lip. His only reported comment after the round was, "Well, I didn't miss many." But he did, in fact, miss a couple of short putts on the front nine—his 33 could have been a 31.

Picard traveled to the Masters with Smith, and the two of them had discussed which was the better position—a stroke or two ahead or a stroke or two behind. Smith, perhaps remembering the pressure he'd faced from out front last year, believed it was better to be a little behind; Picard argued for being in the lead. Now he had his wish.

But breathing down his neck, just a stroke behind, was the tournament favorite. What's more, Sarazen had put together his 68 with a dazzling display of ball-striking and an unhelpful putter. He let a truly great score slip through his fingers by missing six putts in the three- to seven-foot range.

"It was one of the greatest rounds of golf I have ever seen," said Armour, who played with Sarazen in one of the feature pairings. "It matched the greatest golf I have ever seen Harry Vardon or Bobby

Jones play. It was a masterful piece of golf art. After reaching the green, Gene could have used his foot and kicked the ball in for a 65 or 66. . . . I was only one over par, and yet in this round I felt like a hacker."

Sarazen said that, except for those missed putts, he had never played a better round. This from a man who had shot a 66 in the final round to win the 1932 U.S. Open.

A United Press report stated that Sarazen's second shot on the eighth hole "may stack up as the best of the tourney." As it turned out, Gene would hit a shot on Sunday that made this one pale by comparison, but the first-round shot might have had a higher degree of difficulty than the one that would go down in golf lore as one of the greatest ever. After pushing his drive to the right he found his ball lying in knee-high rough (there was some tall grass on the course in the early days of Augusta National) and behind a stand of trees. Sarazen pulled out a mashie (equivalent of a five-iron) and hit a towering shot over the trees, leaving a short third shot to the par-five green to set up a birdie. Another moment of excitement came when he chipped in from 30 feet for a birdie on the 16th. Sarazen was yet another player who bogeyed the 18th, failing to get up and down from the sand and making his only bogey of the round.

All this happened after an odd incident in the wee hours of the morning. Sarazen was awakened by the sound of an intruder in his room at the Forrest Hills-Ricker hotel at around 4 AM He looked up to see a woman peering at him from the foot of his bed. Asking what she wanted, Sarazen got no reply. When he raised himself up on his elbow to get a better view, the woman hastily went out the door, saying, "I beg your pardon, but I'm in the wrong room."

Sarazen grabbed a driver and chased the intruder, who fled down a staircase. "It was the queerest experience I ever had," Sarazen told Rice. "But I was thinking of the forty dollars I had left on my dresser.

These are tough days. I can use that forty dollars to feed my four cows [on his Connecticut farm.]"

Ray Mangrum, joining Sarazen one stroke behind, was one of the five players added to the field based on leading in scoring average on the winter tour among previously uninvited players. While five might have been too many, it did provide a path for younger players. Mangrum was twenty-four, near the beginning of a career that would net him five victories (a total eventually surpassed by his younger brother Lloyd). Also making the field off their winter tour performances were the next two U.S. Open champions, Sam Parks and Tony Manero.

Willie Goggin, runner-up to Sarazen at the 1933 PGA Championship, used an ace on the 16th hole to help shoot his 68. Craig Wood, the Masters runner-up the year before, hadn't played particularly well on the winter tour but perhaps the return to Augusta was good for him as he shot a 69.

A quartet of very good players followed at 70: Paul Runyan (the 1933 and '34 money leader), Johnny Revolta (who would lead the 1935 money list), Olin Dutra (1934 U.S. Open champ), and Jimmy Hines (opening with a 70 for the second straight year). The tenth player to break par on the day, all alone at 71, was Byron Nelson, who was just a few months away from his first tour victory.

They were all chasing Picard, a modest man but one who was now playing with confidence. He grew up in Massachusetts and learned the game as a caddie at Plymouth Country Club. Impressed with the way Henry hit the ball, the pro, Donald Vinton, asked him if he wanted to come south and work with him at his winter club, Charleston Country Club in South Carolina. Just shy of his eighteenth birthday, Picard agreed, with the consent of his father.

That was in the winter of 1925-26, and Henry never went back to Massachusetts. Vinton asked him to stay and run the pro shop in the summer, and Picard took over as head pro five years later when Vinton retired. Charleston remained Picard's home for most of his life, but he spent 1934 to 1940 as the pro representing Hershey (Pennsylvania) Country Club on tour.

The Picard family pronounced the name Pick-ARD, but for the folks in Charleston it naturally flowed off their tongues as PICK-erd, which was all right with Henry. Decades later Picard was asked the pronunciation before being introduced at an event, and he said Pick-ARD. Frank Ford, a very good friend who had known Picard for all those decades, was standing nearby and exclaimed, "I'll be damned! You never told me that." That's how unassuming Picard was.

Ford was one of the top amateurs in South Carolina and a member at Charleston Country Club when Picard arrived. When the eighteen-year-old assistant pro suggested a change in Ford's swing, Ford replied, "Henry, we've played six times and you haven't beaten me yet. I don't want to hear any more."

It took a while for Picard to develop as a player, though he entered some tour events when the circuit moved through the Southeast. One of those was the 1930 Savannah Open, where Picard not only played but also turned into a spectator to watch Bobby Jones play one round. Picard was so impressed with Jones's flowing swing that he decided to adopt a similar action, which required lengthening his swing.

He didn't get it right immediately. Picard broke four four-woods from hitting the ball off the heel and found himself shooting in the 80s for a couple of weeks. Then one day he saw his good friend Ford.

"Frank, I can't play anymore," he said.

"Let me see you hit some," Ford replied. After taking a look, Ford said, "Keep that swing, you'll be great."

Picard stuck with the swing, and eventually it paid dividends.

Even when the new swing clicked in, Picard could only occasionally beat Ford, who would say, "When you beat me three out of five times, you'll be ready for the tour."

That finally happened in 1934, so Picard hit the tour in earnest. He finished 23rd in the first Masters and won the North and South Open the next week. He got a break that summer when the Hershey Company was looking for a tour pro to promote its golf resort. The idea was to create publicity by having the pro listed as representing Hershey, so they needed to find somebody who would play well enough to be mentioned prominently in the newspaper reports every week. Hershey wanted to hire Ky Laffoon after he won the Hershey Open, but he wasn't interested and suggested Picard.

Henry got the job, and it worked out great for both sides. Picard quickly became one of the best players on tour, and the writers not only referred to him as being from Hershey but sometimes by nicknames such as the Hershey Hurricane or the Candy Kid. On his side, Picard got a $5,000 contract, which along with $3,500 from Spalding freed him to play the tour without any financial worries. Winning first prize at Agua Caliente, his hometown event at Charleston, and Atlanta in the first three months of 1935 helped, too.

Picard continued his assault on Augusta National on Friday, shooting 68 for a 36-hole leading total 135 that was far lower than anyone expected—and this was on the heels of shooting a 65 on Monday to win in Atlanta. Picard now seemed in firm control of the Masters, going into the weekend with a four-stroke lead over Sarazen and Mangrum.

Picard had earned the lead even though he missed three short putts in his second round and found the water with his tee shot on the par-three 12th. A fine pitch and a putt there enabled him to escape with a bogey that put him at even par for the day. He followed by hooking his tee shot into the woods on the par-five 13th, but came out into the fairway, hit his approach close, and made a birdie—the first of four consecutive birdies that opened up his margin on the field. He preserved his lead by making a par on the 17th from the same road that had cost Smith a double bogey a day earlier.

Still, Jones's round once again received more attention in the newspapers. This time it was more justified, as he created the day's biggest buzz with a 33 on the front nine, even if he did come back down to earth by going three-over on the back to finish with a 72.

The former emperor engendered his first roar from the gallery by holing a 50-foot birdie putt up and over the big swale on the fifth green. Two excellent wood shots gave him an eagle chance from 12 feet on the eighth, but the whir of a movie camera spoiled the moment. After asking for quiet—in a polite tone, of course—Jones missed the putt. It was still a birdie, and he got another on the par-four ninth with a nine-foot putt.

Word spread quickly and Jones's already large gallery grew. Even the players were getting the word that Bobby had toured the first nine in 33.

Keeler couldn't keep his mind from racing. "And just for a moment there was at least one old golf reporter who was wondering what would happen, if the Jones boy of 1930 should suddenly step into the picture with a 66," he wrote. "But it was merely a fleeting glimpse—a vague and vagrant idea, and a curiously definite ache under the wishbone."

Jones gave the shots back very quickly, thanks to a drive into the woods at the 11th and three-putts at the 13th and 14th. Fours on the last four holes, including a birdie and a bogey, got him home with an even-par 72.

"He isn't the golfer he was but he still is the man he was," wrote McGill, admiring the way Jones gathered himself to fight to the finish after his troubles early on the back nine.

While to the fans it might have seemed that the Jones magic had returned, Bobby knew that wasn't the case. In fact, he felt lucky to have escaped with a 72.

"I was hitting the ball far better in the first round," he said. "I might as well have had a 70 then, in place of the 74, and an 80 today, in place of the 72."

Jones was playing with Sarazen in yet another spotlight pairing. Sarazen lost ground to the leader on this day, making bogeys at the first and 18th after drives into the trees and at the fifth on a three-putt. He managed to shoot a one-under 71 for the day thanks to birdies on all four of the par fives, including the eighth hole where he and Jones both had eagle attempts from 12 feet but couldn't convert. Sarazen's round left him four behind Picard along with Mangrum, whose 71 included an eagle on the 13th.

Olin Dutra and Jimmy Hines held steady Friday, both shooting 70 for the second straight day. Dutra produced the shot of the day, drilling a fairway wood into the wind from 250 yards on the second hole to within six feet and sinking the eagle putt. The *worst* shots of the day were hit by Frank Walsh on the eighth hole. His repeated attempts at recovery from the trees kept smacking into pines and rebounding toward him. Finally, he played out backward and ended up making a 12 on the hole.

Craig Wood slipped a bit with a 72 for 141, followed at 142 by Runyan (70-72), Goggin (68-74), and Walter Hagen (73-69). The Haig told McGill that he did it despite not feeling so chipper before his 11:42 tee time, as his friends persisted in entertaining him and so he had been up until dawn or later the last four mornings. "The friends of the Haig are trying to arrange it so that he will get no sleep tonight," McGill wrote.

How much sleep would Picard be able to get with the lead? Would he be tossing and turning as he thought about trying to repeat Smith's feat of leading after each round?

Picard undoubtedly knew, as did Keeler, that there was too much golf remaining to say that he had the tournament wrapped up.

"All Picard has to do is keep on doing it, and nobody will collar him. But whether you know it or not, that is the very hardest thing to do, in all the gamut of tournament golf," O.B. wrote. "I think it's still a battle, with at least nine battlers in it. And a great tournament."

# 14

# 1935 ROUND 3/THE SQUIRE AND THE BLOND BOMBER

---

**T**HE PAIRINGS COMMITTEE DECIDED to send all of the leaders out in the afternoon on Saturday, teeing off within an hour of each other (though not in consecutive twosomes or inverse order based on scores as is done today). It proved to be a wise move, as it meant all the contenders had to face the unpleasant weather conditions that arose that afternoon.

Just like the first year, Masters weekend brought weather that was anything but what the Chamber of Commerce would have ordered. At least it was warm this time, with the temperature in the 70s, but a wind and rainstorm hit a little before 2 o'clock. The worst of it lasted for about an hour, starting just when Jones was teeing off, with play continuing through the mess.

The weather was just one thing that turned this into a very unpleasant, and unlucky, day for Henry Picard. The leader was assigned to the last twosome, playing with Lawson Little, so he played the first part of his round in the storm.

He also played it in an agitated state, for when he got to the course he found that his heavy niblick (equivalent to a wedge) was missing. Its absence cost him dearly on the third hole, where he had to use a different club for a tough pitch shot, which he knocked over the green, leading to a double bogey. Picard proceeded to miss the next two greens, chip poorly, and card a pair of bogeys that sent him to four-over for the round after just five holes.

The weather eased up and Picard seemed to recover, playing the next 10 holes in two-under. But after a two-putt birdie at the 15th, Picard became undone again. The 16th, at 145 yards, was shorter than today, and guarded by a stream instead of a pond. Statistics showed it to be the easiest of the par threes and fours at Augusta National, but Picard hit a poor tee shot that found the water and made his second double bogey of the day. He followed that with a bogey on the 17th, and even with a birdie from 15 feet on the 18th Picard trudged off the course with a very disappointing 76.

Late in his life, reminiscing with his son Larry, Picard said that he simply ran out of gas after playing in every event on the winter tour, including the two that were held in the eight days before the Masters.

Picard started the day with a four-stroke lead, and finished it two behind. The new leader was Craig Wood, who charged to the front with a 68. It might have been the best round of the week, considering the conditions, as the course yielded only four subpar rounds Saturday, compared to ten on Thursday and fourteen of Friday.

Wood used his length off the tee to advantage on the par-five second hole, where a birdie resulted from him being the only player to reach the green in two all day. His long putting was even more impressive, as he holed three putts of 25 feet or more.

The "Blond Bomber" made a couple of bogeys after hitting tee shots into the woods but pulled off spectacular recoveries on other holes to keep the round together. A bold player, Wood recovered nicely from a failed attempt to reach the par-five 15th in two, saving par after hitting his second shot into the water.

Olin Dutra moved into second place with his third straight round of 70. "He was hitting the ball magnificently today," Jones wrote for a newspaper article. "There were times when I thought he was using a rifle." Observers agreed that all three of the 1934 U.S. Open champion's rounds could just as easily have been in the 60s.

"If there is such a thing as the accumulation of a margin of luck, he should have a bit on his side, Sunday," wrote Keeler. "But that, of course, is the least tangible of all the intangibles of competitive golf, which are numerous and perplexing."

Sarazen lost some of his sharpness as he slipped to a 73 and fourth place on a leaderboard that showed Wood 209, Dutra 210, Picard 211, and Sarazen 212. It looked to be between those four players unless either Walter Hagen or Denny Shute, tied for fifth at 214, could summon a charge.

Shute, whose tour play was limited but was always a threat in the big events, shot a 70 for the third subpar score on Saturday. The other was turned in by Lawson Little, whose 70 moved him to the head of the amateur field and all the way up to eighth place at 216. Little sat just behind Ray Mangrum, who shot himself out of title contention with a 76 for 215.

Jones shot 73, a reasonably good score under the conditions, leaving him in a tie for 15th at 219. It was another day when he made a couple of long putts but missed a couple of short ones, including the shortest yet, from just inside a foot on the 17th.

"I was still not sure of any shot in a tight place where I might need control. And once again my putting fell away," Jones wrote in a newspaper column. "I have now realized that golf, or tournament golf, is a game that needs a lot of competition. It isn't a matter so much of shot making as it is of nerve and muscular control, and this can only come from battle out on the course."

Considering the quality of the leading quartet, Jones didn't see anybody else catching up. "All four are quite capable of breaking 70 and if one does, no one else will have a chance," Jones wrote.

Wood headed into Sunday trying to maintain his lead and end a string of runner-up finishes in big tournaments. It started when he was defeated by Shute in a 36-hole playoff for the 1933 British Open and continued in 1934 with a one-stroke loss to Horton Smith at the Masters and an extra-hole defeat to Paul Runyan in the final of the PGA Championship. Making the close calls worse was that Wood had never won a major title.

The thirty-three-year-old Wood was in the prime of a fine career that had seen him collect a win in every year since 1928, usually two or three. He was a strong player who during the 1933 British Open at St. Andrews had hit a wind-aided tee shot 430 yards on the par-five fifth hole. "That this happened, there is no shadow of a doubt," wrote famous British golf writer Bernard Darwin. "As to how it happened, I give up."

A suave and handsome fellow, Wood had married New York socialite Jacqueline Valentine just after the 1934 Masters. Wood was the pro at Deal Country Club in New Jersey, but the couple also kept an apartment at the Park Lane Hotel in New York City where he cut a dashing figure in city social life.

Wood grew up in Lake Placid, New York. His father, Charles, was six-foot-eight and 275 pounds, a forester who supervised the lumbering operations of the J.J. Rogers Company. Charles owned large tracts of land and the family had enough money to send Craig to prep school in Massachusetts and then to college, first at Clarkson in New York and then Rider in New Jersey. But Wood got into golf the same way as his more hardscrabble comrades, by caddying as a youngster.

Wood got his first pro job at a nine-hole course in Kentucky, and worked in the winter as a bookkeeper and at a tobacco warehouse. He won the 1925 Kentucky Open at the age of twenty-three, but wasn't able to start competing as a regular on the winter tour until 1927-28 when he started working at the Forest Hill Field Club in New Jersey.

Wood's first win of national importance came at the Oklahoma City Open in 1929, a year after the seven-years-younger Horton Smith scored *his* first win there. Wood proceeded from there to the West Coast, hopped on a ship, and beat Smith at the Hawaiian Open. He was on his way.

Now in pursuit of his biggest title, Wood was being most closely chased by a man who had already won two majors. Another big man at 6-foot-3, 230 pounds, Dutra had claimed the 1932 PGA Championship and 1934 U.S. Open. Dutra wasn't as long a hitter as Wood, but few topped his combination of distance and accuracy.

Dutra wasn't a full-time tour player, as he concentrated on his club-pro duties for the bulk of the year—that's why he had missed the first Masters. While other pros had summer jobs at clubs in the Northeast and Midwest that enabled them to play the winter tour, Dutra worked year-round in the Los Angeles area, first at Brentwood Country Club and then at Wilshire Country Club.

Dutra was a Californian through and through, his ancestors having been among the first Spanish settlers in the territory. He grew up in Monterey and learned the game mostly by playing in an open field with his brother, Mortie (who finished 11th in the 1934 Masters), and the five Espinosa brothers (two of whom, Al and Abe, grew up to play the tour). They played with battered old clubs collected from the pro shop at Del Monte Country Club, where they caddied.

Olin quit school at fourteen to work in a hardware store, his income giving him the resources to play on real courses and improve his game. He also would get up as early as 4 AM to practice before going to work. His dream was to get a job at a club, which he finally accomplished at the age of twenty-three in Fresno.

Three years later, Dutra landed a position at Brentwood. He won the Southern California PGA at twenty-seven, but competed little outside of his home state until 1930, when he was twenty-nine. He led the 1932 U.S. Open by four strokes after the first round, but fell back quickly and ended up tied for seventh. Dutra overcame that disappointment with his PGA Championship victory later in 1932 and by coming from eight strokes down over the final 36 holes to win the U.S. Open two years later.

Dutra claimed that title despite an attack of dysentery that hit him on the cross-country train trip, leaving him able to eat very little during the championship. He won by one stroke over Sarazen, who climbed onto the shoulders of his caddie beside the 18th green to watch Dutra attempt a long putt on the 15th. Hopeful of a three-putt by Dutra, Sarazen instead saw Olin hole the putt to send him on the way to becoming the first Californian to win the U.S. Open.

Dutra was a placid personality, of whom George Trevor wrote in *Literary Digest* after the U.S. Open, "You admire Dutra, but you can not love him or hate him—the two emotions from which box-office drawing power is compounded" and that "he lacks the egocentric showmanship of Hagen, the magnetic personality and the lyric artistry of Jones, and the chip-on-the-shoulder cockiness of Sarazen."

Sarazen did exude a confidence that often came across as cocky. He was good, and he didn't mind telling you about it.

But he did it in a manner that didn't rub people the wrong way, according to Trevor. "Gene has the knack of boasting without giving hearers the impression that he is a swashbuckling fire-eater. There is a quiet, ingenuous matter-of-factness about Sarazen's boasts that disarms listeners."

As for the chip on the shoulder, Sarazen was very sensitive to anything that could be perceived as a slight, which he then used as motivation. An example was the 1933 PGA Championship, before which Tommy Armour said that Hagen, Sarazen, and Armour were washed-up as tournament golfers.

"I understand that Tommy will be here for the last few days of the tournament [Armour failed to qualify for the event]. I would like nothing better than to be playing top notch golf and have him here to see with his own eyes that Sarazen can still play golf," Sarazen wrote in a newspaper column, before going out and winning the championship.

Sarazen had an active mind, though it lacked a filter. For example, he wrote in *PGA Magazine* in 1934 that pros shouldn't take their wives with them on tour. "Those women are the curse of golf today. Take the average one of them, who pursues her husband, a good golfer with a good chance to get somewhere in an important championship. Every time he goes to make a shot—a shot that may win or lose the title or a thousand dollars—he sees his wife staring at him with these words in her eyes: 'If you miss this shot and let Mrs. Bloke's husband beat you, why . . .'

"The poor guy may have a fighting heart like Jack Dempsey's, but who can blame him for getting the shakes? He misses the shot and gets a dirty look. Women like that are so strong psychologically that they beat their husbands and turn golf tournaments into 'hen' sessions. Oh, I know. Many a time I've heard a wife give one of my victims a piece of her mind."

Another example of Sarazen unfiltered came at the 1935 Masters, where he told Ralph McGill that the young players on tour played "pansy golf. They get on the greens and they say, 'Oh, it's a little slow,

Paul,' or 'It's a little fast, Charles.' In my day, we didn't tell anyone anything. If the green was fast we hoped they wouldn't find it out until it had cost them some strokes. And the only thing we hoped about the other fellow was that he'd break both legs.

"That sort of spirit made golf. I think maybe the kids are being too polite and are killing off the old spirit."

When he wasn't complaining about something, Sarazen could be quite engaging. He was a fountain of ideas, many of which he floated to his golf writer friends. One of those was to enlarge the hole to a diameter of eight inches, a suggestion which actually led to a tournament being played like that.

Whichever side he happened to be displaying at a particular time— crotchety, charming, clever, or creative—it all worked very well to keep golf, the tour, and himself in the newspapers.

"Sarazen speaks his mind and, what makes it important is that he has a mind to speak. Which is not true of a lot of people who go about speaking their mind," McGill wrote.

By 1935, Sarazen was often speaking out as a member of the old guard. This might seem odd, since he was only thirty-three years old, but he had been around for a long time by then. He burst on the scene in 1922 by winning the U.S. Open and PGA Championship and had been a presence ever since.

Sarazen was born February 27, 1902, making him a contemporary of Jones, who came into the world eighteen days later. Born Eugenio Saraceni in Harrison, New York, just north of New York City, Gene was the son of an Italian immigrant carpenter father. The family didn't have much money, which didn't inspire Gene to want to become a carpenter, though his dad wanted him to take up the trade.

Gene came down with emphysema when he was fourteen years old, such a severe case that he was near death in the hospital for several days. He had already dropped out of school and was working in

Bridgeport, Connecticut, helping to make barracks for use in World War I. When he got out of the hospital, he was told that factory work wouldn't be good for his lungs.

Sarazen had caddied at the Apawamis Club as a youngster and was inspired by the victory of Francis Ouimet—a 20-year-old caddie—in the 1913 U.S. Open. Gene and his friend Ed Sullivan (yes, *that* Ed Sullivan) used to play their way from their homes to Apawamis on an improvised cross-country course.

When he was sixteen, Sarazen made a hole-in-one at a public course in Bridgeport and got his name in the newspaper. Thinking that "Saraceni" sounded like a violinist, not a golfer, Gene gave it some thought and came up with the name Sarazen to use the next time his name would be in the paper—and he did plan on there being a next time. He liked it even better when he checked some phone books and found no one with that name. It wasn't done to disguise his Italian heritage. Sarazen was proud of that, and when he became famous newspaper articles nearly always referenced him as an Italian. (An *Augusta Chronicle* article the week of the 1935 Masters called him "the squat Italian shot maker.")

Sarazen worked for a while at Brooklawn Country Club, but mostly he was sweeping out the pro shop and learning to make clubs. What he really wanted to do was practice, so he would arrive very early and hit balls. His playing talent made him popular with the members, and sensing that the pro didn't like that, Sarazen decided to take off. At the age of seventeen, he boarded a ship in New York headed for Jacksonville, Florida, with no definite plans.

The gregarious youngster met some people aboard ship who took him to Sebring, in central Florida. From there he met the pro at Lake Wales Country Club who let him play and practice. Sarazen was only five-foot-five, but he had developed a powerful game and made a great impression on those who watched him. Some of the club's members gave him money to play in a tournament in Jacksonville on the fledgling pro tour, a not yet fully organized conglomeration of events for professionals.

Sarazen continued on to play a tournament in Augusta, Georgia, at Augusta Country Club, which at the time still had sand greens. That's where he collected his first check (for $50), two weeks shy of his eighteenth birthday. The tournament wasn't exactly what we think of as representing tour golf today. It was a one-day, 36-hole event with a field of less than thirty players and Sarazen earned the money for tying for the low second round, a 73, while finishing tied for fifth with a 152 total. He also met Charlotte Country Club pro Bill Goebel, who offered him room and board and the opportunity to team with him in betting matches to win some money.

Six weeks later, at a tournament in Asheville, Sarazen met a pro from Fort Wayne, Indiana, who gave him an assistant pro job, so it was on to the Midwest. The members there encouraged him to enter the 1920 U.S. Open at Inverness in Ohio, where he finished tied for 30th at the age of eighteen.

The whirlwind advance continued with a pro job in Titusville, Pennsylvania, a pairing with Jones in the 1921 U.S. Open ("I said to Jones, 'We'll make a bet. Every time you throw a club you're going to pay me ten dollars and every time I throw a club I'm going to pay you ten dollars,'" Sarazen later recalled about the pairing of teenagers who still had tempers), a trip south for the 1921-22 winter tour where he won the Southern Open, and another pro job at Highlands Country Club near Pittsburgh.

Sarazen made connections there, too. Since Highlands was just being built, Emil Loeffler, the pro/greenkeeper at Oakmont Country Club, let him play there at one of the toughest and best courses in the country. Sarazen sometimes played with Oakmont founder W.C. Fownes, who helped set Gene up for an early practice round for the

U.S. Open at Skokie Country Club, outside Chicago, a month before the championship. The well-prepared Sarazen won that U.S. Open with a gambling birdie on the par-five 72nd hole giving him a one-stroke triumph over Jones and John Black at age twenty.

For good measure, Sarazen won the PGA Championship, which was at Oakmont that year. Suddenly, he was a national sensation.

The only blemish on that PGA win was that defending champion Hagen wasn't in the field due to his exhibition schedule. In fact, Sarazen nearly missed the event himself because he was playing an exhibition in Ohio on Sunday and didn't realize that his opening match was scheduled for Monday. He hopped on a train and arrived just in time—actually, a little bit late, but they delayed his starting time to allow him to play. They would do that for a marquee player then, and Sarazen was an attraction since he had just won the Open and was a local besides.

Sarazen took care of any remaining doubters the next year when he beat Hagen in the PGA Championship final thanks to a spectacular pitch shot from long grass near the out-of-bounds line that finished inches from the hole. That championship was at Pelham Country Club in New York, where Sarazen's father watched him play for the only time, from outside the fence for just one hole.

For good measure, Sarazen defeated Hagen in a highly publicized, specially arranged 72-hole match, after which Gene was rushed to the hospital with appendicitis. Throughout the rest of the 1920s, he played in a mix of tournaments and exhibitions, making good money for a golfer of that time.

"I never made my living from tournament golf," he said later. "I had to go out and play exhibitions, make appearances, and travel all over the world to keep myself in the public eye."

He might have considered exhibitions his bread and butter, but Sarazen did play a lot of tournament golf in the late 1920s after a heavy exhibition schedule from 1923 to 1925. Sarazen won fifteen tournaments in the decade, but no majors after the 1923 PGA Championship.

Some claimed he experimented too much with his swing. It can't be said that he ever went into a real slump, but his play dropped off enough from that early peak that he didn't really challenge Jones or Hagen (who won four straight PGA Championships starting in 1924) for preeminence in the Twenties.

Sarazen played his fullest tournament schedule ever in 1930 and came away with eight victories for the year, including the Western Open—but was overshadowed by Jones's Grand Slam. Three wins followed in 1931, but it wasn't until 1932 that he regained the major touch.

That's the year that he reeled off a double just as impressive as his U.S. Open-PGA sweep of 1922, winning both the British and U.S. Opens. He won the British using the first modern sand wedge—not the concave-face one that had been banned, but one of Sarazen's design with a flange on the bottom to help the club slide through the sand instead of digging in. He had his equipment company, Wilson, make one especially for him and the 1932 British Open was the first time he, or anyone, used it. Most pros enthusiastically adopted the sand wedge, though some complained that they didn't require any skill. "It would be a wonderful thing for golf if the USGA would bar these trick-shot clubs," Al Espinosa said at the 1935 Masters.

Next for Sarazen was the U.S. Open, where he found himself seven strokes back with 27 holes remaining. Throwing away the cautious strategy he had used to that point, Sarazen tore into Long Island's Fresh Meadow for a 32 on the back nine of the third round and a closing 66 to win by three.

"From the beginning of his career . . . Sarazen has ever been the impatient headlong player who went for everything in the hope of feeling the timely touch of inspiration," Bobby Jones wrote after the championship. "Gene Sarazen is not the kind of player with whom caution agrees. He likes to hit the ball hard off the tee and, when playing an iron, he will always prefer to force a weaker club than ease off on a stronger one. An amazing firmness and boldness even in his short pitches is a characteristic of his game."

Sarazen added a third PGA Championship title in 1933, but tournament play took a backseat that year and the next as he spent most of his time touring with Joe Kirkwood, cashing in on his renewed fame after his Open double. He only returned in January 1935 from the world tour that had caused him to miss the Masters the previous March.

In the early years of the Depression, Sarazen and his wife, Mary, had foreseen rough times ahead. "We decided that the only future in America was to buy a farm and live off a farm," he later recalled. So, they bought a small dairy farm in Brookfield Center, Connecticut, complete with a few cows.

The Sarazens ended up not needing to live off the farm, but they kept their cows and enjoyed their peaceful life in the country so much that it remained their home for thirty-five years. Whereas most of the pros in the 1935 Masters were identified as being from the town of the club they represented, Sarazen no longer was affiliated with a club and was listed out of "Brookfield Center, New York" (a mistake, since it was actually in Connecticut). While Sarazen's farm was no grand estate, his country home nonetheless earned him the nickname "The Squire."

It was attached to him by Grantland Rice, who shot one of his "Sportlight" movie shorts at Sarazen's farm. Rice, incidentally, was once a member at Apawamis, where he sometimes had young Eugenio Saraceni as his caddie.

"Little Gene was a keen, alert, hard-working caddie who was liked by everyone," Rice remembered in an article for *Sport*.

Now Rice was a member of another prestigious club, and writing about the playing exploits of his former caddie. Would Gene give him a good story on Sunday?

Better than anyone dreamed.

# 15

# 1935 ROUND 4 AND PLAYOFF/THE SHOT HEARD ROUND THE WORLD

---

**S**UNDAY AT THE 1935 Masters dawned bleak, cold, wet, and windy. The rain would mostly hold off during the afternoon, but the temperature barely climbed out of the 40s. Just like the previous year, the final round would be played in uncomfortably raw conditions.

It could have been worse. That same day, tornadoes swept through Florida, Alabama, Mississippi, Louisiana, and Texas, killing thirty-four people.

In the chill but relative calm of Augusta, Bobby Jones was, as always, paired with another high-profile player, this time with new amateur sensation Lawson Little. They teed off at 11:00, enabling spectators to follow them for at least nine holes before any of the leaders started.

The leading six players were put into three twosomes, but they didn't play consecutively. The 54-hole pacesetter, Craig Wood, went off at 1:00, accompanied by Henry Picard, who trailed by two strokes. At 2:00 came Olin Dutra, one behind, and Denny Shute, five back.

And at 2:24 were Gene Sarazen and his old rival Walter Hagen. It was another nostalgic Sunday pairing for Hagen, who for the second straight year entered the final round five behind while Sarazen trailed by three. They were almost last off the tee. The only threesome of the day (put together because there were an odd number of competitors) went off behind them, but it contained no contenders.

Everyone hoped Jones would better his 13th-place finish of 1934. Instead, he skied to a 40 on the front nine and finished with his worst Masters round, a 78, and ended up in a tie for 25th. It was up to Little to entertain the crowd in that twosome, and he did. The burly Californian took off his right shoe and sock on the 12th hole and hit the green with a remarkable recovery from the water, only to three-putt for a double bogey. But he holed five putts of between 10 and 25 feet and made six birdies in shooting an even-par 72 on a day when only three players broke par and nobody broke 70. The U.S. and British Amateur titleholder led the "Simon-pures" (as amateurs were invariably called by newspaper writers) by a wide margin and finished sixth overall at even-par 288.

After yielding so many low scores on the first two days, Augusta National bit back on the weekend, even if the miserable weather did most of the work. But the sopping wet course and bitter cold couldn't quite explain all the problems the leaders had on the front nine. None of them seemed to bring their game with them for this most important round.

Wood shot a 39 that could have been even worse if not for a couple of par-saving putts. His playing partner, Picard, didn't take much advantage, posting a 38 that picked up only one stroke and left him one behind. Wood's closest pursuer entering the round, Dutra, fell to pieces with a horrendous 42, dispelling the idea that he was due better luck.

Sarazen was over par, too, but he was the best of them with a 37. Starting nicely with a birdie on the second hole but falling back with bogeys on four and nine, he was within one stroke at the turn.

The back nine was a different story. The wisdom—intentional or otherwise—of reversing the nines was shown by the drama that unfolded on that piece of ground. The reason for the change was so players wouldn't have to face potential disaster on the water holes early in the round, but the back-nine holes also offered plenty of potential for heroics. And heroic performances abounded down the stretch in the second Masters.

Dutra showed admirable resilience on the back nine, shooting a 32 which set the competitive nine-hole record. Since he trailed by four at the turn, that was potentially good enough to win the tournament. It didn't work out that way, so instead of a comeback story for the ages the reigning U.S. Open champion settled for third place at 284 after his 42-32 round of 74. Picard finished fourth after a 75, and Shute fifth with a 73.

Wood three-putted the 10th hole for a bogey, missing from two feet, and parred the next two holes, then put together a closing kick that appeared to win the Masters. He used his length to reach the 480-yard 13th in two and made a birdie. He birdied the 14th with a 12-foot putt. He made it three in a row by pounding two fine wood shots to collect another two-putt birdie on the 485-yard 15th.

The charge stalled with a three-putt bogey on the par-three 16th, but Wood was still in front. And he appeared to apply the *coup de grâce* on the 18th, where after a fine approach shot on the 420-yard par four he holed a 16-foot putt for his fourth birdie on the last six holes and a 34 on the back nine. His 73 gave him a 282 total and he retired to the clubhouse, receiving congratulations along the way for his likely victory.

Out on the course, Sarazen had bogeyed the 10th hole to drop to two-over for the day and two-under for the tournament. He followed with pars on the next two holes. Wood's birdie on the 18th got him to six-under, eliciting a cheer that could be heard by Sarazen and Hagen on the 13th fairway. Even while numbering far fewer than today, the enthusiastic spectators were making enough noise to alert players that something had happened elsewhere on the course.

But *what* had happened? Sarazen didn't know yet, but he knew that when Wood finished some spectators and reporters would rush down to his twosome to see him finish—and carry with them the news of what score Wood had posted.

Meanwhile, Sarazen knew he hadn't caught his drive on the 13th well enough to go for the green in two. Against his nature, but with good judgment, he elected to lay up short of the creek. He was rewarded for his patience with a birdie, as he pitched his third shot onto the green and made a six-foot putt to get to three-under

Sarazen hit a poor drive on the 14th, a low hook that didn't travel very far and also left him with trees in his way. It was at this time he got word that Wood finished six-under. Five holes remaining, and Sarazen would have to play them three-under to tie. This on a rain-soaked course on a frigid day when subpar scores were few and far between. And he was in trouble on the hole he was playing.

Hagen looked at Sarazen and shook his head. "Well, Gene," he said, "that looks as if it's all over."

"Oh, I don't know," replied Sarazen, his expression carrying a slight grin but more a look of bulldog determination. "They might go in from anywhere!"

It certainly was over for Hagen, who was on his way to shooting a 79. Once the Haig was out of it, he was in the mood to reminisce about old times, like how he had sent a wheelchair out to Sarazen on the course at the 1933 U.S. Open and Gene had tried to return the favor at the British Open.

But Sarazen didn't want to get too deeply into the nostalgia, as he was still trying to win the tournament he was in. And he had to bear down on his second shot to the 425-yard 14th, or it really would be over. Aiming for the right side of the green in order to stay clear of the trees, Sarazen made solid contact with a long iron from the rough. He found the putting surface, but was 80 feet from the hole on one of the toughest greens on the course. His first putt stopped six feet away, and he made the next one for a par.

Now there were four holes left, and Sarazen needed to play them three-under. He figured the 15th and 16th holes were birdie chances, but getting one on either of the last two holes would be tough. Then again, if he could get home in two on the 485-yard, par-five 15th and make an eagle, one birdie would be enough.

Gene smacked a drive that came to rest in the fairway a little more than 250 yards from the tee. It was a good poke with 1930s equipment on a wet fairway on a day that seemed more fit for penguins than golfers. It offered him a chance to gamble on clearing the water in front of the green with his second shot and possibly make an eagle.

But not as good a chance as he had hoped. When Sarazen reached the ball, he found it was on a downhill lie and sitting down in the grass besides. He was 230 yards from the hole, a distance from which he would normally hit a three-wood. But he and his caddie, a lanky black man nicknamed "Stovepipe" for the tall silk hat he always wore, agreed that from that lie he wouldn't be able to hit the ball high enough with a three-wood to carry the water hazard.

Sarazen had an answer in the form of a four-wood—not just any four-wood but a special Wilson Turf Rider with grooves on the bottom of the club designed to enable the player to dig the ball out of difficult lies. The problem was that the distance to the hole was a little too far for a four-wood. So Sarazen decided to "toe the club in" a little bit, that is close the clubface slightly, to squeeze out the extra yards he needed.

Sarazen was normally a very fast player, one of the fastest in the game. But with the importance of the situation, the difficulty of the lie, and the consultation with Stovepipe, he was taking a while to hit this shot. "Hurry up, will ya, I've got a date tonight!" Hagen yelled from across the fairway.

Gene still wasn't *quite* ready yet. Remembering the ring in his pocket, he took it out and rubbed it on Stovepipe's head for luck. "I suppose the real contribution the ring made was that fooling with it tapered off the tension that had been building up in me," Sarazen later wrote.

He had plenty to be tense about. This was a high degree of difficulty shot. The lie, the closed clubface, and the distance of the carry over water made it risky. In a different situation, even Sarazen probably would have laid up. But, considering the unlikelihood of making three birdies on the way in, it was worth the gamble.

Sarazen turned to the gallery guard behind him on the fairway and said, "Push 'em back, sonny," and then finally made the do-or-die swing. He knew immediately he had made great contact and had no doubt the ball would clear the water. But the margin for error was so slim that it still didn't clear the water by much, bouncing just short of the green. (There was a bit more room between the hazard and the green than there is today. The pond hadn't been created; instead the green was guarded by a wide portion of a creek.)

Just as impressive as the distance of the shot was the direction. The ball took off straight at the flag and never deviated from its course. As the ball bounced once onto the green, took another small bounce, and started rolling, there was applause and a murmur of anticipation from the gallery. The murmur turned to cheers as the ball rolled closer to the hole—and then to bedlam as it rolled *into* the hole for a double eagle two. Needing to go three-under to tie, Sarazen had done it with a single stroke!

Striding forward to get a better view, Sarazen strained to see the final result. When he saw fans jumping up and down and shouting around the green, he knew what he had done. "They might go in from anywhere," indeed.

"The scene that ensued not only beggared description but put it through a forced receivership. Certainly I am not going to try it on the typewriter," wrote O.B. Keeler, who witnessed the shot from close behind Sarazen. "I walked along with Gene a few rods of his triumphal march toward the green and now the grin on his face was a real grin, and no mistake. But he had nothing to say. He held that little No. 4 spoon somewhat as if it had been a scepter."

Jones was one of the lucky people who witnessed the shot. He had stayed around the clubhouse for a while after completing his round two-and-a-half hours earlier, but decided to stroll down and watch his old friends Sarazen and Hagen finish, just picking them up as they played the 15th. "That was one golf shot that was beyond all imagining, and golf is largely imagination," Jones said that evening. "From duffer to star we all dream of impossible shots that might come off. This one was beyond the limit of all dreams, when you consider the surrounding circumstances. I still don't believe what I saw."

"It was the greatest thrill I've ever had in golf, or ever expect to get again," Sarazen told Grantland Rice after the round. "When I saw the ball cover the flag I knew I had a putt for an eagle three. I hoped it would be a short one. I was afraid of the lie I had, afraid I couldn't hold the right line. I was so tickled when it covered the flag that I couldn't think of anything else until I heard that roar from the crowd around the green. Even then I couldn't believe the ball had slipped into the cup from 230 yards away. . . . When that wild howl went up, I felt for just a second like crying."

Craig Wood must have felt like crying, too, for a different reason. So must Mrs. Wood, who was hoping for a victory to celebrate their first wedding anniversary. The couple had enjoyed the toasts to Wood and his nearly certain victory offered by Augusta National members in the clubhouse, but Jacqueline Wood was nervous and went out to the press area to get word of what was happening on the course.

With her hands shaking, she waited for the report on the short-wave radio that had been set up to relay scores to the press. Suddenly, she and the reporters heard a yell from the crowd out on the course. A yell that wouldn't stop, but just kept on going.

Then a voice crackled on the radio. It said that Sarazen had made a two on the 15th. People wondered if they had heard correctly. Had the man had misspoken? Maybe he said the 15th hole when he meant the [par-three] 16th? He was asked to repeat the information. The voice came —yes, it was a two on the 15th.

Jacqueline Wood was upset. But she quickly remembered there were three holes remaining, and Sarazen would need three pars to tie. Out on the course, it didn't take Sarazen long to get over the thrill and realize the same thing.

"After that I had to hole two tricky four-foot putts and I was still afraid I would blow both and spill everything," Sarazen said that evening. "I honestly think those last three holes were the heaviest pressure I've ever known in golf. I knew if I missed one after that [double eagle] two I would be just a mug."

Sarazen gave himself a birdie chance at the 16th, but missed from 12 feet. He holed his first tricky four-footer at the 17th. The uphill 420-yard 18th was one of the toughest holes on the course, and Gene made it even tougher with a poor drive to the left similar to the one he hit on the 14th. The hole was open to that side, so Sarazen had a clear shot. But he had gone the opposite way from the dogleg, lengthening a hole that already played long because it climbed the hill to the clubhouse.

Sarazen normally had a five- or six-iron into this green, but he was so far back that he pulled out the same four-wood he had used on the 15th hole. He struck the ball straight and true yet again, the ball landing in the vicinity of the pin and rolling some 30 feet past.

He faced a treacherous downhill putt, however, so getting down in two was no guarantee. Eleven years later, Ben Hogan would three-putt from 12 feet above the hole to lose by one. Sarazen gingerly stroked his 30-footer, which rolled so slowly that he practically was walking alongside the ball as it approached the hole. Somehow it stopped four feet short, leaving a knee-knocker to force a playoff.

"Too much analysis would be a bad thing in that spot, I decided," Sarazen later wrote. So he stepped up and hit the putt without taking any extra time. The ball dropped, and Sarazen's highly improbable comeback was complete. He had made a playoff.

Jacqueline Wood hugged her husband. "We'll get him tomorrow," she said.

It was absolutely amazing that there was a tomorrow. Even in the game as it is played by the long hitters of the twenty-first century, there are generally only a couple of double eagles in an entire year on the PGA Tour. In the 1930s, they were an even rarer bird.

What were the odds of a double eagle? Somewhere in the vicinity of tens of thousands to one. What were the odds of a double eagle being scored by a player who was three strokes behind with time running out in the final round of a tournament with the importance of the Masters? Incalculable. That's why, even more than seven decades later, it is still considered the greatest shot in the history of the game, all circumstances considered.

Of course, there was an element of luck in holing out a shot from such a long distance.

"I may not have been aiming for the cup from 230 yards, but I was aiming at the flag. I had to. Only a perfect shot would do there," Sarazen wrote in the *Saturday Evening Post* shortly after the tournament. "Lucky? Oh, yes, quite lucky. But it was a good shot, hit exactly the way I wanted to hit it."

And Benito Juarez had nothing to do with the luck—as Sarazen discovered only when he read his friend Bob Davis's article in the June 1935 issue of the *American Golfer*.

But the Turf Rider club, introduced by Wilson just a year before, *did* help Sarazen pull off the shot. Sarazen had a couple of them with him in the fall of 1934 when he was about to head to Australia and New Zealand for a leg of his tour with Kirkwood. On the way, he played a round or two with Brian Bell, a friend who was the Southern California editor of Associated Press.

Bell noticed the distinctive club, which Sarazen explained was different not only because of the grooved sole but because it had a little more loft than a traditional spoon. Sarazen called it a "wooden cleek," meaning that it had the loft of a cleek (the equivalent of a one-iron) but was a wood club. Equipment companies had just started using numbers instead of names for their clubs, so the Turf Rider was a four-wood while the club formerly known as a spoon was a three-wood.

Sarazen, seeing his friend's interest, told Bell he could take the extra one.

As related in John Olman's book *The Squire: The Legendary Life of Gene Sarazen*, when Sarazen returned from Australia, he phoned Bell.

"Do you still have that wooden cleek I gave you?" he asked.

"Sure," Bell replied.

"Well, someone swiped mine in Australia," Sarazen told him, "and if you'll give it back, I'll make you a present of three matched woods.

They were made for me, but I can't use them. They're an ounce too light."

So Sarazen got back the club he would use for his historic shot.

As to what happened to the club *after* the shot, that's a mystery. Sarazen told his family that he gave away the special club during a trip to Japan in 1937. He later gave a club to Augusta National for display in the clubhouse, telling them it was the double eagle club. And after the 1939 St. Paul Open in Minnesota he gave a Turf Rider four-wood and a seven-iron to his caddie, a teenager named Thor Nordwall.

A story in the next day's *Minneapolis Star-Journal* reported that Sarazen said he gave his caddie his "famous three-wood [sic]" from the 1935 Masters in appreciation for his services. "He's the best caddie I've ever had," Sarazen was quoted as saying.

But Gene didn't tell Nordwall that it was the club from 1935; Nordwall thought Sarazen might have given it away because he was disgusted with the club after a poor shot on the 18th hole of the final round. Nordwall put the club in his own bag and used it for years. He hadn't seen that newspaper article, but he'd been told about it, and in 1970 he found it on microfilm in the library. In the 1980s, he decided to try to return the club to Sarazen, but Gene never responded. In 2008, Nordwall donated the club to the USGA museum.

Alas, it's probably not the club Sarazen used for the double eagle. It has a patent number on the bottom; the club from 1935 would have been stamped PAT. PENDING because the patent wasn't issued until 1936. It also has Do-Do on the leading edge of the sole. Sarazen referred to his double eagle as a "dodo" to emphasize its rarity, and later versions of the four-wood were given that label. So the only way this is the club is if those markings were added later, which is highly unlikely.

You also have to wonder why Sarazen would have given away such a meaningful club to a caddie who carried his bag at one tournament (which he didn't even win) and who he would never see again, without even telling him it was *that* club. Or, for that matter, why he would give it away in Japan.

It makes more sense that he would have given it to Augusta National. But Sarazen might have already given away the real club by the time he gave a four-wood to Augusta in 1949. Augusta has admitted that it doesn't know if the club on display is the one Sarazen really used. Late in his life, Sarazen said he wasn't sure himself what happened to it.

Adding to the confusion, Wilson made a number of replicas of the famous club either for Sarazen or for its own promotions in the late 1930s, and Gene probably gave away some of *those*, too.

Another important club for Sarazen that week was the putter, which was one he picked up after arriving in Augusta. Before heading out for his first practice round, Gene told Augusta National pro Ed Dudley, "Someone has stolen the putter I used to win the British and American Opens in 1932, and I can't putt with any other." Dudley suggested a new model, which worked like a charm. When word got around, Dudley did a brisk business selling the putter in his pro shop.

Sarazen's 70 on Sunday was the best round of the day. There were only two rounds of 71, shot by a pair of players—Clarence Clark and Mortie Dutra—who started the round far out of contention. Sarazen produced a clutch 33 on the back nine to do it and played the last six holes in four-under.

When McGill congratulated him after the round, Sarazen told him, "Well, the crowd paid $2.20 each and they deserved some entertainment."

How many of that crowd witnessed the double eagle? Newspaper estimates of two thousand made by Rice and nearly all news outlets can be dismissed out of hand. There probably weren't even that many on the entire grounds. As discussed earlier, the 1934 attendance was not much more than a thousand people a day. Roberts said later that the attendance was down for several years after the first Masters. Keeler, on the other hand, wrote that the Sunday gallery was "vastly increased" from the inaugural Masters. But even if more people did come out for the final round, that wouldn't account for two thousand people gathered on the 15th hole when Sarazen played it.

Later in life, Sarazen himself always said that only twenty people witnessed the shot. That seems to have become the accepted number, but we shouldn't look at his estimate uncritically. Sarazen was a great storyteller, and the dramatically low number was probably his way of embellishing the tale. (He liked to contrast it with the twenty thousand he said had told him over the years that they witnessed the shot.)

There must have been more than twenty for them to make enough noise for McGill to hear them from the clubhouse and for Keeler, who was on the 15th fairway, to write that the celebration was so wild that it "beggared description." Unfortunately, Keeler didn't mention how many people took part in that celebration.

In his reminiscing, Sarazen spoke of counting the number of people around the green. Certainly there were others standing in the fairway behind him. Luther Stafford recalled in 2004 to *The State* newspaper in Columbia, South Carolina, that as one of the 16-year-old gallery guards from Richmond Academy he was holding one end of a bamboo pole in the 15th fairway to keep the crowd back from Sarazen as he swung.

With Sarazen playing in the penultimate group, the crowd wouldn't have been very dispersed as he neared the end of the round with an all-but-empty course behind him. When Sarazen was making his double eagle, Dutra was coming up the 18th hole, so some of the crowd would have been there. But other than that, there weren't any players of note still on the course to see. (Byron Nelson was in the twosome ahead of Sarazen, but he was a little-known player at the time.) Word had undoubtedly gotten around that Sarazen was the only player with a chance to catch Wood. Jones came out because he was curious to see Sarazen and Hagen finish, and others must have had the same idea.

My best guess: There were probably a hundred people around the green and at least a couple hundred altogether who witnessed the shot.

Sarazen's spectacular finish didn't win the tournament for him, of course. It merely got him into a playoff the next day. If he didn't prevail on Monday, the double eagle would end up being just a footnote to history—a major footnote, but a footnote just the same.

The Masters followed the U.S. Open's lead in having a 36-hole playoff. Most tournaments used an 18-hole playoff; the longer Masters playoff was perhaps meant to signal that this was a really big event. The morning round was scheduled to start at 10:00, with the second round set for 2:30 after a lunch break.

Wood and Sarazen made for quite a contrast. Wood was tall and muscular; Sarazen short and stocky. Wood was one of the friendliest guys on tour, known for giving younger players a helping hand. Sarazen was more combative, and sometimes rubbed people the wrong way with his outspokenness. Wood had a track record of finishing second in the big events; Sarazen had won two U.S. Opens, a British Open, and three PGA Championships. Two similarities: both were thirty-three years old and had grown up in New York state.

The weather didn't improve for the playoff. Overnight rain left the course more soaked. The temperature, in the 40s when play started, never climbed above 55. "April in Georgia, and there we were blowing on our hands to keep them warm," Sarazen later recalled.

The Atlantic Coast Line announced Sunday evening that it would extend its special overnight train service to the Northeast an extra day to accommodate golf fans staying to watch the playoff (the special train had been scheduled to end Sunday because that was considered the end of Augusta's winter season). It appeared, however, that most fans didn't change their plans. Only an estimated four hundred—if that many—showed up for the playoff.

They saw a tightly fought battle for nine holes turn into a Sarazen golf clinic for the final 27. Both players shot even-par 36 on the front nine in the morning, but the first four holes of the back nine told the tale. Sarazen picked up one stroke on all four holes, making a birdie from 20 feet on the 10th and watching Wood bogey each of the next three. Wood pulled his approach on the 11th to where the pond is today; it stayed dry because there was just a stream there in those days but he couldn't get up and down. He then sent his tee shot onto the bank beyond the green on the par-three 12th and hit his first and third shots into the water on the par-five 13th, where he had to one-putt just to make a bogey.

Joe Williams figured Wood was beaten even before he teed it up in the playoff.

Having a nearly certain victory snatched away by Sarazen's double eagle, Williams wrote, "might be likened to a bettor who had drawn a sweepstakes winner but lost his ticket on the way to the pay window. Wood realized then, as everyone else did, that this wasn't his tournament. He was merely a medium through which the gods of sport decided to satisfy a capricious whim. All along Sarazen was destiny's choice."

Once he got the lead, Sarazen became a relentless par-making machine. After making three birdies and two bogeys on the first 10 holes, he ground out a remarkable twenty-four straight pars, giving Wood little chance of a comeback on another day that was not meant for low scoring. Sarazen was in the rough only four times and didn't visit a single bunker in 36 holes.

"I look back on my playoff rounds as constituting some of my finest golf. Certainly I was never straighter," Sarazen wrote in *Thirty*

*Years of Championship Golf.* "My play that entire week at Augusta, for that matter, was my best tournament effort since 1932, no doubt about that."

Sarazen led by four strokes, 71-75, after the first extra round. Any hopes Wood had of a comeback were wiped out early in the afternoon round as he missed par putts of four and three feet on the first and third holes and also bogeyed the fifth and seventh. Now Sarazen was eight strokes ahead and it was all over but the shouting. Wood shot a 34 on the final nine, but it was far too late. Sarazen won by five strokes, 144-149.

Jones was impressed. "Once Gene Sarazen makes up his mind he's in position to win a tournament, he is the hardest golfer in the world to beat. He started this tournament with superb confidence and his confidence never left him, even when he seemed hopelessly beaten in the final round."

The tournament founder and course co-designer had to be pleased with the drama provided by Sarazen's double eagle, especially as it was made possible by Jones's philosophy of making the par fives reachable in two shots.

Wood's overall performance in the playoff must have been disappointing, not only because he finished second in yet another big tournament but also because he squandered what O.B. Keeler called "one of the finest day's work off the tee I have ever seen, for combined range and accuracy." Sarazen was considered a fairly long hitter, yet Wood consistently outdrove him by 20 to 40 yards with long carries netting him impressive distance on the wet fairways. But Wood's iron play and putting let him down badly, and he was runner-up at Augusta for the second year in a row.

At the awards ceremony, Wood again accepted a check for $800 for second place. It was reported on the Associated Press wires that he also received a check for $500 from Augusta National member

Alfred S. Bourne, who had picked Wood in the tournament's Calcutta pool.

The extra dough (he and Sarazen also received $50 for going an extra day in the playoff) didn't go far to salve Wood's wounds, as he couldn't hide his disappointment when asked to speak a few words at the ceremony. "Last year I lost the championship because Horton Smith holed out two long putts," he lamented. "This year I lost it because Gene Sarazen holed a 220-yard putt. Next year I suppose they will be sinking even longer putts."

The movie cameras were rolling when Sarazen accepted the $1,500 winner's check from Rice. (They also got footage of Sarazen holing a six-foot par putt on the final playoff hole. Not the actual putt—he was asked to repeat it three more times for the movie cameras, and made it every time.)

"It is with the greatest of pleasure that I present this check of first-place money to Gene Sarazen, one of the greatest golfers in the world today. Outside of being one of the greatest golfers in the world, I also think Gene is one of the luckiest," Rice chuckled, referring to the double eagle. "I think Craig Wood after hearing of that deuce should have taken a rifle and gone out there on the fifteenth and shot Gene through the heart. I don't believe a jury would ever convict him for the deed."

Called to the microphone, Sarazen began, "Perhaps I was somewhat lucky to win this tournament. But that brings up a question. When you miss a seven-footer the crowd says it's hard luck, but when you hole the same kind of putt they simply dismiss it by saying you're lucky. So there you are.

"I have enjoyed playing in this tournament very much and believe that the Augusta National has a tournament that is next to both the National Open and National Amateur, from the standpoint of interest and competition. And I hope to be back next year."

Sarazen also showed his feisty side. "You know, when I came here for this tournament they all said the 'old timers' didn't have a chance against a field of such stars," he continued, ignoring the fact that he and Jones were the favorites. "Well, you see I had to uphold the reputation of Bobby Jones, Walter Hagen, and myself."

While upholding his own reputation, Sarazen enhanced the reputation of the Masters. It was a feather in the tournament's cap for a player of his caliber to win it, and the *way* he took the title raised it to another level. The return of Bobby Jones in the inaugural Masters made it the most talked-about tournament of the year, and the thrilling second act featured one of the most extraordinary shots and remarkable finishes in the history of the game.

In just two short years, the Masters had established itself as American golf's rite of spring. By now it had dawned on everyone that Jones would probably not be a threat to win his own tournament. But the tournament was already past *needing* that. The writers would continue to come and the articles would continue to be placed at the top of the nation's sports pages to tell whatever stories happened to develop at Augusta National.

The Masters was not only off the ground, it was flying high. Nothing could stop it now from taking its place in the pantheon of golf tournaments.

# 16

# 1935 POST-MASTERS AND BEYOND/ TRIBULATIONS BUT MAJOR STATUS

O R COULD IT?
Only four days after the end of the 1935 tournament, Clifford Roberts wrote an extraordinary letter to Augusta mayor Richard Allen, stating that the Masters wouldn't be held next year without financial support from the city, and complaining about the cut in support from $10,000 to $7,500 in the second year. The following week, he released the letter to the *Augusta Chronicle*.

"Our second tournament was . . . distinctly successful and I believe it can be made far more popular in the future if it is continued along the very same lines that it was handled this year. I must state very frankly, however, that the leading taxpayers of Augusta and the business interests generally, must come forward and see to it that an adequate tournament fund is made available. In my opinion, it was a serious mistake to cut the appropriation from $10,000 to $7,500, as this resulted in a shortage of money for the various activities that are vital to the success of the tournament. I refer particularly to advance publicity, advertising in Florida, radio, etc.," the letter read.

"What I am really proposing is far sighted planning and a little better team work all around. The small group that has seen fit to join and to support the Augusta National has all it can do to keep the club going. We are unable to hold the tournament again if there is to be any question about a substantial sum being made available by the city or its agency."

Essentially, Roberts was threatening to take his ball and go home if the city didn't give him what he wanted.

As justification for the funds, he cited the boost the Masters gave to Augusta by increasing business during the tournament and in publicizing the city as a winter destination. Roberts offered a "suggestion" for how the city should proceed in order to avoid the criticism that had arisen from parts of the citizenry the last time money was appropriated for the Masters. It should make a survey of the taxes generated from property owned by winter visitors and "institutions that depend on the tournament for patronage," determine the percentage of those taxes needed to maintain or increase the present amount of tourist business, and give that amount to an independent committee of businessmen to distribute as it saw fit.

There's a good chance Roberts was bluffing about not holding another Masters. While it was true that the tournament benefitted Augusta, it also benefitted the club. The Masters, after all, was created to raise the club's profile and attract the members it desperately needed to boost its struggling bottom line. It was still needed for that purpose even if the tournament wasn't making a direct profit and the purse money had to be collected from individual members. Would Augusta National really call a halt to a tournament that brought national attention to a club that was looking for national membership?

Roberts tried to strengthen his position by writing that "our president, Mr. R.T. Jones, Jr., concurs in the thoughts I wish to suggest to you," realizing that Jones's name carried more weight than his own.

The letter must not have gone over too well. Funding of $7,500 (not $10,000) wasn't approved until January 1936, and then only after a debate. The city ignored Roberts's suggestion of how it should proceed, instead appropriating the money in the same way as before.

The club played the bluff, it that's what it was, all the way to the end. It didn't announce the 1936 Masters until January 11, after the city money was approved.

Roberts was keeping a low profile by that point. The story announcing the Masters said that Fielding Wallace was the general chairman of the tournament and that Innis Brown of the *American Golfer* was tasked with assembling the field, "a responsibility which formerly was borne by Clifford Roberts." The tournament committee consisted of Fielding Wallace, W.H. Wallace, Lansing B. Lee, Jerome Franklin, and Montgomery Harison, with Alfred S. Bourne as an ex-officio member. Officers of the club were listed as Robert T. Jones, president; Bourne, vice president; Jay R. Monroe, secretary; and Fielding Wallace, treasurer. Was Roberts busy in New York during this winter season? Or had the presumptuous tone of his letter to the mayor made him such an unpopular figure that the club preferred not to list him as being involved with running the tournament (though undoubtedly he was in control behind the scenes)? The latter seems more likely.

This was but one of many storms the tournament and club weathered through the remainder of the 1930s. Augusta National went through foreclosure. Tournament attendance did not pick up. The bad luck with weather continued. Financial support from the city ultimately ended. Augusta stagnated as a winter destination. The Depression continued.

Still, none of this materially affected the prestige of the Masters in the eyes of the players or the press. Not even the considerable problems of its host club could stop the Masters.

Starting a golf club and building a golf course during the Depression had proven to be an untenable venture, even with Bobby Jones's name and Clifford Roberts's savvy behind it. The club simply had not been able to attract enough members to be able to pay its bills. It still owed $25,000 in construction costs and hadn't been able to keep up with its mortgage payments.

Just two months after the high of a thrilling 1935 Masters came the low of foreclosure. But it wasn't a disaster for the club. In fact, it was a way out. In those economic times, there wouldn't exactly be a lot of bidders for a golf course when Georgia Railroad Bank put the property up for sale after foreclosing. So, a group of five Augusta National members was able to buy it for $30,000 in June 1935. They then formed a new entity, the Augusta National, Incorporated.

Meet the new club, same as the old club—except that it was now free of obligations to its old creditors, as the original club had officially gone out of business. In December 1935, the club wrote a letter to the creditors and underwriters stating that although there was no legal or moral obligation to make any provision for them, it had decided to offer them Class B stock in the new corporation based on the amount they were owed. Well, it was better than nothing—if this version of the club fared better than the original.

The new Augusta National was able to start with a clean slate instead of a mountain of debt. The embarrassment factor was minimized as the transactions were not written about in the newspapers, although the legal notice of the foreclosure did appear in the *Chronicle*.

The club was still very much in need of members, but building up the roll remained a slow process. In 1939, Roberts wrote a letter to the members exhorting them to help find desirable candidates for membership. With each copy of the letter he enclosed several membership applications for the members to hand out. In 1940, the club's ninth year, it finally reached a hundred members.

The next year, *Chronicle* sports editor Tom Wall led a column by listing the names and hometowns of five new members who had just joined Augusta National. "For his $385 membership fee each of the new members received a share of stock," he wrote. "For his $66 yearly dues, the new member got only a receipt."

In announcing the addition of the members, the club proudly stated that it brought the total membership to 135. It was still a long climb to the approximately three hundred members that would constitute a full slate—and decades before the club would reach the point where its membership rolls were shrouded in secrecy.

Still, the membership gains, along with the 1935 restructuring, put the club on sounder financial footing. That was a good thing, since in 1937 the city decided to stop funding the Masters.

One reason was an increasing discontent each year with Augusta National's request for funds. It was one thing to help get the Masters off the ground, but there was growing opposition to city funds being used for an apparently successful event run by a private club. More specifically, the January 1937 denial of Augusta National's request was due largely to the efforts of one man, William E. Bush, president of the Forrest Hills-Ricker Hotel.

Bush's objection was that Augusta National had not submitted to municipal officials any report or audit of how the money it received in the last three years was used. He threatened to enjoin the city council if money was appropriated for the Masters, and Mayor Allen and Chamber of Commerce secretary Lester S. Moody let the matter of a request for $4,000 in funding drop without bringing it up for a vote.

According to the *Chronicle's* Wall, the city of Miami tried to swoop in with a $75,000 offer to bring the Masters there. The tournament said no. In truth, it made no sense for the tournament to leave Augusta, no matter what the offer. The Masters was inextricably linked with Bobby Jones's Augusta National Golf Club; taking it somewhere else just wasn't in the cards.

Not one to give up easily, Roberts (by now back in his public role as tournament and club chairman) made another request to the city for funding for the 1938 tournament. That one was swatted away quickly in September 1937, Mayor Allen telling the finance committee that the tournament made money last year and he didn't think city money should be spent that way.

The year 1939 proved to be a turning point in ticket sales. Previously, the focus was on attracting winter visitors, which was in line with the near obsession with the tournament's role in promoting Augusta as a winter destination. It wasn't until the sixth year of the tournament that somebody had the bright idea to intensively market the Masters to locals. That somebody wasn't from Augusta National, it was an Augusta businessman named Alvin M. McAuliffe.

Clifford Roberts in his 1976 book *The Story of Augusta National Golf Club* wrote of the tournament's early years that "a very small percentage of [Augusta's] permanent residents had any interest in either playing golf or watching the game played. Neither the large percentage of black citizens nor the millworkers could be expected to do very much about supporting a golf tournament."

That might have been true, but Roberts was underestimating just how many people in a city of sixty thousand *could* support a golf tournament, especially in an era when a couple thousand people constituted a very good crowd.

It was McAuliffe who appreciated not only what a good thing Augusta had in the Masters, but that the local community could play a vital role in the tournament's health. He formed the Business Men's Masters Tournament Association for the expressed purpose of selling Masters tickets at various local businesses.

"The businessmen of Augusta realize the benefits of the tournament and want to assure its continuance here from now on," McAuliffe said. "They want to make the tournament a financial success by increasing the interest of those living in the surrounding area."

The association canvassed various sections of the city, enlisting businesses to sell Masters tickets. The goal was to sell two thousand season tickets (the prices, incidentally, were the same as in 1934—$5.50 for a week-long ticket, $1.10 for practice rounds, $2.20 for tournament rounds).

Even with a late start—the association was formed just over two weeks before the tournament—the local sales helped the Masters top its 1934 gate for the first time. And it got even better in 1940. After that tournament, Roberts credited the Business Men's association for doubling ticket sales in the two years of its existence. The locals had saved the tournament's bacon.

The business community continued to play a key role in selling tickets and promoting the tournament through the 1940s and 1950s, and attendance rose by leaps and bounds. By 1962, the *Chronicle* was estimating the final-round crowd at between thirty-eight and forty thousand. It's not known how accurate that estimate was, because attendance figures weren't released, but in 1963 the club limited ticket sales in order to avoid overcrowding. By 1966, tickets sold out in advance. Demand grew so high that a waiting list was established in 1972 and closed in 1978.

While the club itself still wasn't keeping its financial head that much above water in the late 1930s, it helped to have wealthy members. The club made three major improvements in the late 1930s and early 1940s, each of the projects funded by an individual member, not by the club itself.

First, in 1937, the 10th hole was lengthened by moving the green back some 35 yards. This was done partly because drainage wasn't very good for a green that was at the bottom of a hill, but also to strengthen a hole that was pretty easy as it was severely downhill for its 430 yards. "It played too short because of the terrain," Jones wrote in 1951. The large bunker that formerly sat to the left of the green has been retained to the present day. While it's not in play for the pros, it is one of the most striking bunkers on the course—the only one to keep the many-fingered look that most of the bunkers had in the early days.

The seventh hole got a similar treatment the next year, its green moved back 20 yards to a new site. The original seventh was inspired by the 18th at St. Andrews, a short par four with a dip in front of the green. But it didn't provide much of a test at 340 yards, and what challenge it *did* provide wasn't a fair one because the green didn't work as the designers intended (at least not as Jones intended; MacKenzie was in his grave, so we don't know what he would have thought). "The contouring of the original green was too severe, or if you choose, too tricky," Jones wrote.

The change to the seventh was suggested by Horton Smith, winner in 1936 as well as 1934. It was carried out by Perry Maxwell, a former MacKenzie associate who was also the architect of the revamped 10th. The new seventh green was placed on a hill, with bunkers dug into the slope at the front. Trees were planted to the left of the fairway to narrow the drive. It made for a hole with a different character than the rest of the course, but variety can be a good thing and most agreed the hole had been improved.

Also in 1937-38, Maxwell made changes to the ninth, 14th, 16th, 17th, and 18th greens and/or the bunkering around them. The original ninth had a very distinctive look with a bunker jutting into the front of the green and a narrow tongue of putting surface wrapping around part of each side. But some players discovered an alternate route on this hole up the first fairway (MacKenzie and Jones wanted players to take different angles into the greens, but this was going too far), and Maxwell completely redesigned the green with five bunkers on the left side and none directly in front. He also added three bunkers in front of the green on the 17th, a hole that originally had no bunkers.

The course changes showed the influence that the Masters had already taken on at Augusta National—nearly all of them were made with tournament play in mind and served to strengthen the course for the pros. (The other big project around this time was a clubhouse renovation in 1941.)

Sarazen had said all the right things about the course being one of the best he'd ever played when he won in 1935, but he later wrote, "On my first visit, I must admit, I was let down by Bob's layout. . . . Bob always made it a point to ask his friends for criticism and I never hesitated to express my honest opinion about holes I thought could be improved. With the assistance of Perry Maxwell and [later] Robert Trent Jones, Bob has continually lengthened and remodeled the holes that were found to be wanting in true shot value. The 10th and the 16th [completely revamped in 1947], which were two of the weakest sisters, are now superb tests of skill."

The tournament continued to produce compelling drama and quality winners. Smith claimed his second title in 1936 by one stroke over Harry Cooper and two over Sarazen. Byron Nelson made up six strokes over Ralph Guldahl in two holes (12 and 13) in the final round to win a battle of young Texans in 1937. Henry Picard atoned for his weekend collapse of three years earlier to win in 1938 and Guldahl enjoyed his moment in the sun in 1939, shooting a 33 on the back nine to nip Sam Snead by one. Colorful Jimmy Demaret won in 1940 and Craig Wood *finally* got his first big win in 1941. The 1942 tournament, the last until the end of World War II, featured the two best players in the game—Nelson and Ben Hogan—in a playoff, won by Nelson.

One downer in the 1930s was an unbelievable run of bad weather. After the cold of 1934 and 1935, two days were washed out by rain in 1936. The tournament was forced into a 36-hole Monday finish played in the rain under conditions so poor that PGA tournament manager Bob Harlow protested. The Masters also had a day's play washed out by rain in 1938 and another in 1939.

Augusta National couldn't control the weather, but was on top of nearly everything it *could* control. Say what you will about Roberts's legendary dictatorial tendencies (which really manifested themselves later in his forty-three-year reign as tournament chairman), he worked hard at making the Masters the best it could be. Players were pampered and made to feel it was a special week. The course was in the best condition of any they played all year. Spectators had free on-site parking, free pairing sheets, their food needs were met, and as early as the 1930s the club began building mounds to provide them with better views. An underground-cable score reporting system, the first of its kind, was installed in 1941. The press was well taken care of, and when the increasing numbers of writers covering the tournament (300 accredited in 1940) outgrew the clubhouse veranda, a press tent was erected.

The tournament drama, the excellence of the golf course, the invitational nature of the event, and the constant improvements implemented by Roberts all helped the tournament maintain the momentum it had created in the first two years. Jones slipped into a role as a ceremonial player (never topping his 13th-place finish if 1934), but the tournament didn't diminish in importance.

There is a tendency, because of the relatively small, informal nature of the early Masters, to believe that it gradually built itself up to major status over the course of its first twenty-five years or so. This isn't really the case. In fact, *all* tournaments were relatively small and informal in the 1930s compared to what they later became.

We've already seen that press coverage of the Masters rivaled that of the U.S. Open from the outset. It also immediately leaped to the top of the players' list of preferred tournaments. Sarazen and a couple of others may have missed the inaugural Masters, but once the tournament was established the top players made sure to be there.

In 1936, the top fourteen players from the previous year's tour were on hand, in 1937 the top nineteen, in 1938 the top seventeen, and in 1939 the top sixteen. The size of the field dwindled into the fifties and forties in those years, but that was because fewer players were invited and marginal ones often stayed away for economic reasons. That in no way diminished the prestige and importance of the tournament.

As early as 1936, the Masters was referred to as a "major" in print. It didn't hold quite the same meaning as today, but was a significant appellation just the same. Lawton Carver, sports editor of the International News Service, wrote in 1941, "The United States Golf Association may not choose to do anything about this situation and probably couldn't anyhow, but the fact remains that the Masters championship is the one that professional golfers are rapidly preferring to win above all others."

Wood won that Masters, and it was hailed as a breakthrough after he had lost playoffs in the Masters, U.S. Open (1939), British Open, and PGA Championship earlier in his career. Wood called it "the happiest day of my life." He would go on to add the 1941 U.S. Open title for good measure.

That Wood's Augusta triumph was called a big win instead of a major one had nothing to do with the Masters stature, and everything to do with the fact that the concept of professional majors hadn't come of age.

Traditionally, the U.S. Open, U.S. Amateur, British Open, and British Amateur were considered the four majors. With the rise of professional golf, that concept would have been outdated even in the

1920s except for the exploits of Jones. The Grand Slam was a construct that applied only to him; the pros weren't eligible for two legs of it and Jones was the only amateur who could regularly contend in Open championships.

Once Jones retired, the Grand Slam became irrelevant. Nobody really thought to replace it, or christen its professional equivalent, until 1960 when Arnold Palmer won the Masters and U.S. Open. It was Palmer's sportswriter friend Bob Drum who said that if he could add the British Open and PGA Championship Palmer would win the modern Grand Slam, and the concept of those four events being the "major championships" stuck.

It stuck because those tournaments were *already* considered the four biggest, even if they hadn't been specifically referred to as "the four majors." The same four would have been considered the four biggest tournaments in 1935, too, the Masters having easily eclipsed the only other contender at that point, the Western Open. And with the attention accorded the Jones comeback, we might as well stretch that back to 1934.

So, the Masters succeeded beyond even the dreams of Roberts and Jones. What about Augusta as a winter destination? That's a different story.

To read the *Augusta Chronicle* you would have thought that Augusta was flying high as a winter destination in the 1930s. Reading between the lines, and with the benefit of hindsight, you can see that the Augusta's tourist trade was actually declining and the city was desperate to hold its position. The Masters came along just when Augusta needed a boost in that regard, and that's why it was embraced so warmly by the city and given public money to help it get started.

The *Chronicle* was fond of stating that Augusta had an "ideal" winter climate (once even calling it "the finest climate in the universe"), while it frequently referred to Florida's climate as "enervating."

But with an average high temperature of 58 degrees in January and the average overnight low of 33 leading to chilly mornings, there were many days when it was too cold to comfortably play golf. As the 1934 and 1935 Masters showed, there were even cold days in March and April.

Florida didn't have that problem, and with rail service getting better and better it became more the "go-to" place for winter golf. By the late 1930s, Augusta was marketing itself as a stopover on the way back to the Northeast in the late winter/early spring for those who wintered in Florida. The Masters fit in with that plan. The problem was that winter-long, not short-stay, visitors, were the bread and butter of the resort hotels. Florida was taking an increasing share of those—and it was an increasing share of a declining number of people who could afford to head south for the winter during the Depression.

There was another problem, pointed out by *Chronicle* sports editor Tom Wall in a column following the 1934 Masters that didn't follow the editorial page's rah-rah line. Sure, the Masters was great, he noted, but other than that Augusta was pretty dull.

"There is nothing here to stimulate activity of such a character as will appeal to the average tourist," Wall wrote. "There is no horse racing. The sport might thrive here if it were possible to carry on legalized betting, but that's taboo. The same is true of dog races. A night club in which guests might spend an evening dancing to the syncopated melodies of a big-time orchestra, take their Martinis before their meals and pay for their fun with real money? Find it. Augusta has climate and Augusta has golf, but the two of them are not enough to keep three winter resort hotels anywhere near full for even a fraction of their season."

Another thing Augusta didn't have—beaches.

As for the resort golf, Augusta couldn't match Pinehurst, North Carolina. The Masters gave Augusta publicity, but the private Augusta

National didn't do much to attract *playing* visitors (though it wasn't hard to get on as a guest in the early days).

The first ominous sign for Augusta's tourist trade was when Vanderbilt pulled out of the Bon Air in 1935. The competition between Forrest Hills and the Bon Air got a little testy around this time. Forrest Hills erected an advertising billboard on Walton Way that blocked the view of the Bon Air, angering not only Bon Air management but neighborhood residents. On Christmas night of 1935, a few men took to the billboard with axes and the next day someone threw saturated rags at the sign, leaving black marks. A crowd of spectators gathered to both boo and cheer when it was cleaned.

The seriousness of the winter hotels' problems became clear when the Bon Air went bankrupt in 1937. It wasn't forced to close, but it never really recovered. Over the next twenty-seven years it had a dizzying succession of owners, being sold in 1939, 1941, 1943, 1945, 1950, 1954, 1962, 1963, and 1964, with various lessees mixed in and additional bankruptcies in 1960 and 1964.

Augusta's winter resort era ended with World War II. The Forrest Hills-Ricker was taken over by the Army in 1942 and turned into a hospital. It never reverted to a hotel, remaining a VA hospital until 1980, two years after the golf course was turned over to Augusta College. The building was demolished in 1988.

The Bon Air changed from a seasonal to a year-round hotel in 1941 and prospered during the war years when many military families stayed there. There was hope when Sheraton took it over in 1945, but neither they nor any of the future owners could make it work. While each new owner claimed something along the lines of, "It is our intention to restore the Bon Air to its former prestige," the decline continued.

Masters visitors found that instead of a heavenly experience, staying at the Bon Air was more like a week in purgatory. That was especially true after the hotel was forced to close due to bankruptcy in 1960—but reopened for a few months around Masters time for each of the next four years.

*Sports Illustrated* writer Dan Jenkins wrote an article lampooning the Bon Air in 1964, and got sued by the new owners who were turning the hotel into a retirement place (which it remains, under different ownership). He was served papers at Augusta National while covering the tournament. Jenkins and Time Inc. ended up winning the case because it was ruled there was no malice intended.

The third resort hotel, the smaller Partridge Inn, went through a similar decline. It managed to remain a hotel and was nicely renovated in recent years—but was sold at foreclosure in 2011.

So, the Masters, through no fault of its own, utterly failed to save Augusta as a winter tourist destination. Yet the city can look at the $25,000 it contributed to the Masters from 1934 to 1936 as a brilliant investment. While it didn't bring seasonal tourists, the Masters grew into a major spectacle that draws a huge influx of visitors for one week a year—visitors who spend a lot of money in the city and provide locals with the lucrative business of renting houses for the week. (Augusta lost its cotton mills, too, from the pre-war era, and never became an inland port, yet the city still boomed after World War II as a medical and military center and the county population is now 200,000. Not quite the quarter million by the mid-1950s optimistically envisioned by the *Chronicle*, but strong growth nonetheless.)

It's striking how many things that didn't work out as intended in those early years served to make the Masters what it is.

The Fruitlands Manor site was available for Augusta National only because the Fleetwood Hotel project was aborted a few years earlier. Had the Fleetwood been built, the site would have turned into another failed Augusta resort hotel instead of the home of the world's greatest tournament.

Augusta National once planned to raze the original clubhouse, but couldn't fund a new one. The building it was forced to keep became one of the iconic clubhouses in the game.

The club wanted to host a U.S. Open. Only when that wasn't possible was the Masters idea hatched.

Bobby Jones didn't want to ever play in a competitive tournament again. But the birth of the Masters forced his hand, because he was needed as a player to make the tournament a success.

The Masters was conceived not as one of the four major championships, but as a way to pull Augusta National out of an economic hole by bringing in members. It didn't work in the short run—the club went under anyway—but it did in the long run.

Augusta backed the tournament thinking it would help secure the city's standing as a winter destination, but just eight years later the resort business was already dead.

Jones and Alister MacKenzie's idea in designing the course was that "severe penalties for one wayward shot should, so far as possible, be eschewed," as Jones wrote. Yet those few holes where penalties are severe—the water holes—are considered the greatest on the course and provide the most excitement in the tournament. The water holes were hidden on the front nine in 1934. The nines were reversed in 1935, but who could have predicted then that the dramatic and beautiful holes of the back nine would someday be beamed in color into millions of homes around the world?

One thing that *did* work out as intended was the potential excitement created by par fives that were reachable in two. But it was a stroke of luck for the Masters that the most famous shot in the history of the game was struck on one of those par fives in just the second year of the tournament.

With due respect to the roles played by the guiding hand of Roberts and the greatness of the golf course, the keys to the success of the Masters were Bobby Jones and a double eagle.

Jones was a near deity after his Grand Slam, and his name alone made the Masters a special event. Most importantly, his comeback as a player spurred such interest that the new tournament was one of the most important golf events of 1934.

Then in the tournament's second year, Sarazen, one of the best players and most colorful figures in the game, won thanks to a blow so monumental it became known as The Shot Heard Round the World.

The magical Jones name and the magical Sarazen shot assured that the Masters started out at the very top in its formative years of 1934 and 1935.

After that, it was just a matter of staying there.

# POSTSCRIPT/
# THE COURSE THEN AND NOW

**T**HE ONLY CONSTANT ABOUT the Augusta National Golf Club course has been change. The layout on which the 1934 and 1935 Masters were contested differed greatly from the one we know today.

Four holes were considerably easier than their modern versions. The seventh, 10th, 11th, and 16th all underwent significant changes within the first eighteen years of the Masters, so their originals are hardly remembered today.

While the course was in some sense easier because of the relative weakness of those holes, it played harder overall based on scoring. Only four players broke cumulative par for 72 holes in 1934 and only five in 1935. Chalk that up to 1930s equipment and greens that were not as smooth as they are today. The course played 6,700 yards compared to today's 7,435, but in terms of what clubs the players were hitting for their approach shots it was effectively longer overall even if a significant number of holes have been lengthened enough to play similarly.

The spoken and written comments of designers Dr. Alister Mac-Kenzie and Bobby Jones in the immediate aftermath of the course's opening always highlighted that the course was designed to be playable for the average golfer and yet challenging for the expert. The same can legitimately be said for the modern Augusta National, but the emphasis has changed. The original was a members' course that could also function well as a tournament course; the modern Augusta National is a tournament course that can also function well as a members' course.

The holes at Augusta National are very familiar to the golfing public these days. The vast majority of that public will never get to play the course, so naturally we tend to think of the holes in terms of the way they play for the Masters. Nearly all of the changes to the course over the years have been made for the sake of the tournament—either to maintain or enhance the challenge for the players or, in some cases, to improve the experience for spectators.

The hole-by-hole capsules below, describing how the holes played in 1934 compared to how they play now, are geared strictly to how the course plays for the Masters. There have been so many changes over the years, it's impossible to cover them all. Concentrating mostly on the 1934 and 2011 versions of the course, I have also mentioned some of the more significant changes in the interim even if those changes have since been altered in turn.

MacKenzie died without ever seeing the completed course. His only description of the holes, written for the *American Golfer*, was prepared before the course construction and was based on preliminary plans. In some cases, his description does not quite match what was actually built. Keeping that in mind, I have used MacKenzie's descriptions when appropriate. (Note: References to the year changes were made refers to the first Masters they were in play.)

### No. 1, Par Four, 400/445 Yards

For a course initially built with only twenty-two bunkers, it's surprising that several of them were put where they hardly came into play. One of those was on the left side of the fairway about 50 yards short of the green on the first hole. That bunker was replaced in 1951 by one to the left of the front part of the green.

MacKenzie wrote that a long, straight drive skirting a group of trees on the right would be in the best position for the second shot. "Long" because a bunker jutting into the right part of the fairway needs to be carried to get there. At one point that bunker became virtually obsolete as everyone could carry it, but with the bunker moved forward and tee moved back the feat is now almost impossible except by the longest hitters with a strong wind behind them. That narrows the landing area for the drive, as do trees to the left that were added in the 1970s.

### No. 2, Par Five, 525/575 Yards

The essence of the hole remains very similar to what it was originally—it's a downhill par five reachable by long hitters, but not everyone, in two shots. It was easier to hit the green with your second shot in 1934 because there was a bunker only on the right. A second bunker was added in 1947 to guard the front of the green on the left, meaning that you can now bounce the ball onto the green only through a narrow opening. But a very long drive to the left of the fairway, catching a downslope, enables the player to carry his second shot all the way to the green, maybe even with an iron.

The original hole had a bunker in the left center of the fairway that had to be carried to shorten the distance on the dogleg left. This bunker may not have been much of a problem for the early pros; it certainly wasn't by 1967 when it was removed and a new bunker built on the right side of the fairway, farther down.

### No. 3, Par Four, 350/350 Yards

The only par four or five that has not been lengthened since the course opened. A single fairway bunker to the left was replaced by a series of four bunkers in 1983, but that didn't change things strategically. The one thing that's different now is that the modern player can get close to the green with a driver. Not many try it, though, because that can leave a difficult short pitch to a plateau green—or if the drive is pushed it can rattle among a group of tall trees that jut in from the right. For most players the only difference from 1934 is laying up with a shorter club off the tee.

### No. 4, Par Three, 190/240 Yards

While he didn't build replica holes, MacKenzie said the original fourth was "very similar" to the 11th (Eden) hole at St. Andrews, with a green guarded by a front bunker but sloped severely back to front so that a safe tee shot left a difficult downhill putt. There was also a bunker to the left but MacKenzie didn't explain the extremely narrow tongue at the left front of the green, which was not like the Eden— perhaps this emerged during construction. In 1937, Perry Maxwell widened the tongue to make it usable for hole locations and also softened the severe slopes of the green somewhat.

The original tee was directly behind the third green; the hole was lengthened by moving it to the right of the green in 1954 and then moving it back 35 yards in 2006. That last move made it play longer and tougher than the original.

### No. 5, Par Four, 440/455 Yards

This was tied for the toughest hole on the course in 1934 because it's long and plays even longer with an uphill tee shot. It's not quite as hard today because the course boundary has kept it from being lengthened enough to keep up with technology, so players are hitting shorter clubs for their approaches. But fairway bunkers were never in play on drives until 2004 when they were pushed back 80 yards. This effectively lengthened the hole a little bit by making players play to the right, but the main difference was in tightening the landing area for tee shots. MacKenzie had a left-side fairway bunker in his plans, but it apparently wasn't built. The bunkers added later were too short to be in play for the pros.

The green was originally bunkerless; a bunker added on the back left is not particularly consequential. The green features a large mound in the middle near the front. In 1934, the top of the mound was at the immediate front of the green but before the next year the green was extended forward to make it easier to run the ball up the slope, a necessity on a long hole for the average player and sometimes for the pros of that era.

### No. 6, Par Three, 185/180 Yards

The distance is basically unchanged (the five yards difference is probably just a matter of more accurate measuring), so today's players are using less club. In 1934, as now, there was a large bunker in front, but it had an odder shape then (true of nearly every bunker on the course). The original green had a large mound in the center, which was flattened in 1938 and replaced with a back-right shelf that makes for a small target when the hole is located there.

### No. 7, Par Four, 340/450 Yards

This hole has had three distinct phases. The original was based on the 18th at St. Andrews, a short par four with a pronounced dip in front of the green, but differed in that the green was deep on the right and shallow on the left beyond the dip. The hole was too easy in a way because it was so short, the only challenge provided by green contouring that Jones later said was more severe than intended.

After just four years, the green was torn up and replaced by a new one 30 yards farther along, on top of a rise. The green was given a different character than the rest of the course by three fronting bunkers, with two more bunkers later added in back leaving a small green ringed by sand. Somewhat later, the tee shot was given a different character, too, the landing area tightened into a narrow corridor by trees that were planted on the left and original small trees that grew on the right. In this phase, it was a long iron off the tee and a pitching wedge to a green that was a difficult target even for that club.

The hole has been transformed in the past decade by moving the tee back twice, ultimately adding another 80 yards. Now if players want to hit a wedge or nine-iron to the green they need to hit a driver and risk missing the narrow fairway, while laying back now leaves a very challenging longer second shot.

### No. 8, Par Five, 500/570 Yards

The fundamentals haven't changed—it's a par five with a blind, uphill second shot; reachable in two only with two long, accurate shots and out of range for short hitters. The period of 1956 to 1979, when the distinctive mounds around the green were eliminated for better spectator viewing, is best forgotten. The green and surrounds have been restored to essentially what they were originally, with no bunkers.

The hole's lone bunker is in the fairway. In 1934, it was in the center of the fairway. It's unclear how easy it was to carry. Accounts of the early Masters don't reveal anyone hitting into the bunker, but do report on a number of players in the trees to the right and the left, so perhaps the sand made them play toward either side. The bunker was eventually moved toward the right but still sits in the fairway. It's now virtually impossible to carry, but a player must flirt with it to be able to reach the green in two; a drive on the left part of the fairway is blocked from the green by trees.

### No. 9, Par Four, 420/460 Yards

MacKenzie's original was unusual and visually striking, a boomerang shaped green bending around a jagged bunker. However, pictures show the ends of the boomerang appearing too narrow for hole locations, so its utility was questionable. What's more, some players were hitting their tee shots down the first fairway for a better angle. So Perry Maxwell redesigned the green in 1938 with four bunkers (now reduced to two) on the left to stop that. The green looks less interesting now, but it plays interesting thanks to a false front.

There have been times when it wasn't uncommon for players to be able to blast drives all the way down the hill for a wedge approach, but that wasn't true at the beginning, nor is it the case now that the hole has been lengthened. A stand of small trees on the right has grown in the seventy-eight years since the first Masters, and more trees were added in this area in 2002.

### No. 10, Par Four, 430/495 Yards

The beautiful bunker about 35 yards short of the green is purely ornamental now, but originally it was to the left of the green. The original green sat in a low area that didn't drain well, and the hole played short because it was severely downhill off the tee, so the green was moved back and onto a plateau in 1938.

MacKenzie's original intention was to reward a player for hitting to the higher right side of the fairway, leaving a good view and an approach unimpeded by the bunker. It didn't end up playing that way for the pros. They were able to hit very long tee shots down a slope on the left side of the fairway, and the bunker—which didn't hug the green—wasn't a hindrance on short approaches. Since the 10th hole was lengthened, it has become a disadvantage to hit to the right because it leaves a very long second shot.

### No. 11, Par Four, 415/505 Yards

The original tee was right of the 10th green, creating a dogleg to the right that played fairly short because it's downhill. There was a bend in Rae's Creek to the left of the green, but if the approach was missed to that side it usually stayed on a wide, gently sloped bank covered with rough. MacKenzie called it "a most fascinating hole," but his description was so short it's not clear why it was fascinating except that it lacked bunkers (there's now a bunker at the back right of the green). It was a pretty easy hole, yielding the lowest scoring average relative to par of any par four in 1934.

Jones installed a small bunker smack in the middle of the fairway after the first Masters, wanting one blind hazard similar to St. Andrews, but it was unpopular and soon was filled in. Big changes came in the first couple years of the 1950s when a dam was constructed, turning the creek into a pond on the left—a much more threatening hazard—and a new tee was built to the left of the 10th green. The main reason for the tee change, which required cutting into a stand of pines, was to improve spectator flow, but the effect was to make it a longer straightaway hole of 445 yards.

By the 1990s, players were hitting short irons into the green. To restore it as a mid-iron approach hole (like its middle period, but unlike the original when it was a shorter approach) the tee has been moved back twice making it now a downhill 505 yards. Once a wide-open driving hole, it was tightened considerably with the planting of pines on the right in 2007. The original hole doglegged around a stand of trees farther to the right, but with driving distances of the 1930s it probably didn't require a fade except perhaps for long hitters.

### No. 12, Par Three, 150/155 Yards

The yardage is about the same, so players had to hit a longer iron with the equipment of 1934. They got a break, though, because the bank of Rae's Creek in front of the green was covered with rough so that a tee shot coming up short didn't necessarily roll back into the water. The front bunker was skinnier than it is today. The one bunker (instead of two) behind the green was on top of a hill and not in play. In the early 1960s the green and swale behind it were raised about two feet to alleviate a problem with wet ground, bringing the back bunkers level with the putting surface and steepening the bank in front. A small creek in front of the tee that drained into Rae's Creek was buried in a pipe to eliminate a flooding problem such as occurred during the rainy 1936 Masters.

The test of hitting a shallow, angled green guarded by the hazard in front has never changed. The back right section of the green was expanded slightly in 1951.

### No. 13, Par Five, 480/510 Yards

The original hole probably played more like 465 yards and was well within range of most pros in two, as is today's version. The essence of the hole was similar—a long drive with a draw around the corner (today's long hitters sometimes hit a three-wood) sets up a second shot to a green guarded front and right by a creek. The hole has been lengthened twice by purchasing property from the adjacent Augusta Country Club to build new tees and keep pace with driving distance, in 1976 and 2001.

The hole had no bunkers when it was built, but before the first Masters four were created to the left of and behind the green. Those were later reconfigured, with one of the new ones replacing a front tongue of the green in 1955. A deep swale to the left of the green was built in 1984; recovery shots from there were so difficult that players became hesitant to go for the green in two, so the swale was moderated in 1988.

### No. 14, Par Four, 425/440 Yards

The original hole had a large bunker in the right-center of the fairway. Like the bunkers on the first, second, and eighth, it's not clear how much they were in play for the pros in 1934, if at all. The bunker was eliminated in 1952; the 14th is now the only bunkerless hole on the course. (The seventh, 11th, 15th, and 17th didn't have bunkers in 1934 but added them later.) These carry bunkers reflect more the Jones philosophy of rewarding a long drive than the MacKenzie philosophy of providing safe routes for the average player—it's the average player who has the narrower target. As on those earlier holes, carrying the bunker afforded the best angle to the green, this time from the right side. An approach from the left was blind and if it was a run-up had to negotiate "a succession of hillocks and hollows," MacKenzie wrote (they are now gone).

The same change was made after 1934 as on the fifth hole, moving the outline of the green forward in order to better enable running the ball up over a large mound. The green, with its wild undulations and overall sharp left-to-right slope, hasn't changed much and provided a large degree of the hole's difficulty, then and now. The original hole effectively played longer with the equipment of the 1930s, which likely accounted for the fact that it was tied for the toughest hole on the course in 1934—or maybe that was an indication that the fairway bunker did come into play.

### No. 15, Par Five, 485/530 Yards

The hazard in front of the green was not as imposing nor quite as close to the green, as it was a creek instead of the pond it became when it was dammed in the 1950s. A hillock to the right of the green, designed by MacKenzie to allow players to sling the ball onto the green, was replaced by a bunker in 1957 at the suggestion of Ben Hogan. This was done to increase spectator safety and to force players to deal with the water. The formation of a pond on the 16th hole in 1948 brought water into play for a severely long shot to the 15th.

By the 1990s, pros were reaching the green with mid- and even short-irons. Lengthening the hole to 530 yards in 2006 restored something close to the original go-for-it equation. A big change in 1999 was the addition of a new stand of trees on the right side and some companion trees to three existing pines on the left of the fairway, tightening what had been a wide-open driving hole.

### No. 16, Par Three, 145/170 Yards

The original tee was behind and to the right of the 15th green, playing to a green guarded by a narrow creek angling across, a shorter carry on the left than the right. This was similar to the 12th hole, but less challenging. The yardage might have been shorter than listed, and the hole was widely considered to be a bit too easy.

A new hole was unveiled in 1948, with the creek dammed to create a pond and the green shifted from the left of the water to the right of it. The tee was moved to the left of the 15th green so the hole still played across water and also was lengthened. However, not many shots find the water today because hole locations on the left side can be reached by aiming right and using the slope of the green.

### No. 17, Par Four, 400/440 Yards

MacKenzie wanted the original shallow green kept so firm that a run-up approach would be "essential" even though the hole was not particularly long. "Until the players have learned to play the desired shot," he wrote, "this undoubtedly will be one of the most criticized holes." Either the hole was not playing as originally intended or Maxwell felt differently, because he installed three bunkers (there are now two) in front of the green in 1938, nearly eliminating the run-up.

An open driving hole gradually turned into a tight one as small trees left standing on the right and left sides during construction grew up to become obstacles (the one on the left is known as the Eisenhower Tree because President Dwight Eisenhower wanted to get rid of it). Pros ultimately were able to hit over them, but the club narrowed the landing area by planting trees on the right in 1999 (the same stand that is in play on the 15th) and the left in 2006. The tee has been pushed back on two occasions since 1999, but the hole still effectively plays a bit shorter than the original.

### No. 18, Par Four, 420/465 Yards

Like the first hole, the original 18th had a bunker well short of the green that wasn't in play and has since been filled in. The two green-side bunkers were in the same position as today, but the one on the right was shaped like the state of Texas. The green had even more back-to-front slope than it does now, but that has been offset by faster green speeds.

Originally, the ideal drive was down the right side, flirting with trees but cutting off some distance on the dogleg right and also giving a better angle for the approach. By the 1960s some pros, including Jack Nicklaus, favored blasting a long drive down the trouble-free left side and still having an approach that wasn't all that long. The club responded in 1967 with two fairway bunkers on the left. A new tee was built 45 yards farther back in 2003, a dramatic change at the time since this hole was lengthened all at once instead of in two stages like many other holes. But it restored the challenge, and strategy, of the hole to something like the original.

Overall, noteworthy developments have been the addition of bunkers, trees, and length. The original design was almost startling in its paucity of bunkers, just twenty-two in all. The course now has forty-four, exactly twice as many as it started with. When the course opened, it had nine holes without greenside bunkers, now it has only two (the eighth and 14th). The process started even before the first Masters when four bunkers were added adjacent to the 13th green. Still, Augusta National has fewer bunkers than most courses.

Trees have proliferated in a couple of ways. Some small trees that were left standing during construction have grown considerably. Also trees have been planted through the years. That includes those added to the seventh hole in the 1950s and the first and 18th in the 1970s, though the biggest proliferation came in the period 1999 to 2007, as noted in the capsules above.

This happened at the same time the course was lengthened dramatically. The added yardage made the course play something like it used to before the distance gains achieved by the pros and amateurs who compete in the Masters, but the trees changed the way Augusta National plays by narrowing the originally wide corridors.

Another change made around the turn of the twenty-first century was growing semi-rough instead of cutting the grass outside the fairways at barely above fairway height as had been done for decades (using the term "semi-rough" because it is not as deep as the rough at most courses). While seen as a break from tradition, this was actually a return to the way the course was set up in the early years. For example, here's how eyewitness O.B. Keeler described Gene Sarazen's second shot on the 14th hole of the final round in 1935: "He tore that ball from the thick rough with a slashing iron shot . . . "

The difference between today and 1934 is that the fairways were very likely wider then. This would have allowed players to favor one side or the other for a better angle on the approach shot, which is part of the strategy that Jones and MacKenzie built in.

Green speeds are dramatically faster than they were for those early Masters, but many of the slopes have been softened in order to accommodate the way the ball rolls on today's shaved surfaces. Putting was probably just as difficult then because the original undulations and slopes built in by MacKenzie and Jones were more severe—which Jones the player may have come to regret.

# ACKNOWLEDGMENTS

**M**Y NO. 1 SOURCE for recalling the world of the 1930s in Augusta, Georgia, was the archives of the *Augusta Chronicle* with its accounts of the founding of Augusta National and the beginnings of the Masters. The newspaper was also an unabashed booster of Augusta as a winter tourist destination and the role the Masters played in it. For tournament reports they supplemented their own staff with articles by O.B. Keeler of the *Atlanta Journal* in 1934 and 1935 and Ralph McGill of the *Atlanta Constitution* in 1935.

The research was much more manageable because the *Chronicle* has a searchable online archive, eliminating the need to pore through microfilm trying to find needles in a haystack. Those archives are managed by newsbank.com. Thanks also to Lisa Kaylor for microfilm research on a couple periods missing from the online archives.

Another important resource was the USGA library, directed by Nancy Stulack. There I had access to 1930s periodicals including the *American Golfer*, *Golf Illustrated*, and *PGA Magazine*, the *PGA Record*

*Book*, and the 1934 Masters program. In addition to its library of periodicals and books, I made use of the USGA's own collection, which includes oral histories conducted with Gene Sarazen, Paul Runyan, and Henry Picard, and the very comprehensive scrapbooks collected by Horton Smith during his career and donated to the USGA.

There are a number of books on the history of Augusta National, the tournament, and the course, the most authoritative being *The Making of the Masters: Clifford Roberts, Augusta National, and Golf's Most Prestigious Tournament*, by David Owen. Others include *The Story of the Augusta National Golf Club*, by Clifford Roberts; *Alister MacKenzie's Masterpiece: Augusta National Golf Club*, by Stan Byrdy; *The Masters: Golf, Money, and Power in Augusta, Georgia*, by Curt Sampson; *A Golf Story*, by Charles Price; *The Masters: Augusta Revisited*, by Furman Bisher; *Augusta: Home of the Masters*, by Steve Eubanks; *The Masters: Golf's Most Prestigious Tradition*, by Dawson Taylor; and *Down Rae's Creek: A Famous Stream at Augusta, Georgia's Fall Line Hills*, by Michael C. White.

For Bobby Jones there are *Golf is My Game* and *Down the Fairway*, by Bobby Jones; *Sir Walter and Mr. Jones*, by Stephen R. Lowe; and *Bobby: The Life and Times of Bobby Jones*, by Sidney L. Matthew. On Gene Sarazen: *The Squire: The Legendary Life of Gene Sarazen*, by John M. Olman and *Thirty Years of Championship Golf: The Life and Times of Gene Sarazen*, by Herbert Warren Wind. On the history of Augusta there is *The Story of Augusta*, by Edward J. Cashin.

Books on other figures: *Gettin' to the Dance Floor: An Oral History of American Golf*, by Al Barkow; *The Velvet Touch*, by Horton Smith and Marian Benton; *Craig Wood, the Blond Bomber: Native Son of Lake Placid*, by J. Peter Martin; and *The Life and Work of Dr. Alister MacKenzie*, by Tom Doak, James Scott, and Raymond Haddock.

On the pro tour: *The History of the PGA Tour* and *Golf's Golden Grind*, by Al Barkow; and *The PGA*, by Herb Graffis.

Other periodical sources (many found in articles in USGA library's clip files) were: *Literary Digest, Saturday Evening Post, Golfdom, Midwest Golfer, Golfer's Yearbook, Sport, Golf Digest, Golf Magazine, Golf Journal, Sports Illustrated, Senior Golfer*, and *Golf Course Management*.

Other newspaper sources from the 1930s were the *New York Times, New York American, New York Post, Chicago Tribune, Chicago Herald and Examiner*, as well as unidentified papers from articles in Horton Smith's scrapbook. I found material from the wire services Associated Press, United Press, and International News Service, and syndicated newspaper columnists Grantland Rice and Joe Williams via Google News Archives, an undertaking which has sadly been abandoned by Google.

Articles from recent years in the *Augusta Chronicle* written by Scott Michaux, David Westin, and John Boyette were helpful as were articles from the *The State* in Columbia, South Carolina, by Bob Gillespie. Other modern sources were golf.com, espn.com, usga.org, and findacase.com.

Also thanks to Errie Ball, the last living participant in the 1934 Masters; Henry Picard's son Larry Picard; and Rob Harris, whose website golfdisputeresolution.com led me to the McWane Cast Iron Pipe Company lawsuit involving Augusta National.

# ABOUT THE AUTHOR

Copyright © by Ron Ramsey

**D**AVID BARRETT HAS COVERED twenty-four Masters, first for the *Augusta Chronicle*; then for *Golf* magazine, where he was a features editor for eighteen years; and also for GolfObserver.com. He presently has his own website, davidhbarrett.com, that is part of TheAPosition.com. The author of five previous books on golf including *Miracle at Merion*, which was awarded the USGA's 2010 Herbert Warren Wind Award for golf book of the year, he lives in White Plains, New York. He is no relation to Thomas Barnett, the prominent Augustan who led Bobby Jones to the site that became Augusta National Golf Club.

# INDEX